on
Knowing

on
Knowing

essays for the left hand

Expanded Edition

JEROME S. BRUNER

the Belknap Press of
Harvard University Press
Cambridge, Massachusetts
London, England
1979

The two lines from William Butler Yeats's "Among School Children"
and the stanza from his "A Prayer for Old Age" are quoted by
permission of The Macmillan Company, New York (*The Collected
Poems of W. B. Yeats,* 1955). The lines from Louis MacNeice's
"Postscript to Iceland for W. H. Auden" are quoted by permission
of Faber & Faber, London (*Collected Poems, 1925–1948,* 1949).
The last chapter, "Psychology and the Image of Man," is reprinted
by permission of Oxford University Press, from H. Harris, ed.,
Scientific Models and Man: The Herbert Spencer Lectures 1976,
© Oxford University Press 1979.

Library of Congress Catalog Card Number: 78-66286
ISBN 0-674-63475-6 (cloth)
ISBN 0-674-63525-6 (paper)

Printed in the United States of America

for Blanche

Preface to the Expanded Edition

There is something unique about the essay form. An essay posits for itself a topic and a set of constraints that limit the forms of comment one can make upon it. If the constraints are violated, the effect is to make the essay somehow slack, unserious, undisciplined. The essay is the literary counterpart of the "possible world" of the logician or like the "thought experiment" of the scientist. As with each of these, it begins with a set of connected familiars and seeks by rearranging them to leap to the higher ground of novelty, a novelty rooted in what was previously familiar.

On Knowing was originally written in the form of separate essays, each of them organized around some familiar matter—the impact of Freud on common sense, the concept of fate, the nature of the modern novel, the role of surprise in thinking, and so on. They were all matters that were "interesting" to me. It is not what made them interesting to *me* that now concerns me, but rather what might make them interesting to somebody else—and my focus is on the nature of intellectual interest rather than, say, upon why these particular matters should have occupied a university intellectual in the late 1950s and early 1960s. For I am fascinated with what it is that makes people try to think through certain issues, whether in an essay, a logically connected possible world, or in a scientific experiment.

As a start, let me propose that interior intellectual work is almost always a continuation of a dialogue. This is not a new point. Its most famous exponent is the Russian psycholinguist Vygotsky, who argues that the development of thought in the child is dependent upon his entering a dialogue and that, in time and with practice, the dialogue becomes internalized. Not that thought consists solely of internal speech—there is ample evidence to warn us off that view. Indeed, even external dialogue is built upon shared, nonlinguistic presuppositions about the world, and these, in turn, are shaped by structures of mind that predispose us to experience "reality" in one way instead of others. Rather, it is the dialectical, almost dramaturgic quality of dialogue that provides a model for pursuing our own thoughts in the privacy of our own consciousness.

Each of the essays in this volume started in conversation. The Freud essay, for example, grew out of conversations with Grete Bibring, Robert Oppenheimer, and Elting Morison. Its preoccupation was with the manner in which a system of thought—however verified it might or might not be by the usual methods of putting a theory to test—could change or, better, crystallize a generation's mode of thought. My partners in dialogue were a psychoanalyst, a physicist (whose sympathies were very much with Freud although they were buffered in doubt), and a historian whose lifelong concern has been the relationship of power and ideas within a society. Each was a strong-willed protagonist. And in each conversation, the inevitable happened. By the very dynamics of dialogue you are constrained in two ways: first, you come to take the positions of the other rather for granted, and after a while it becomes an unfriendly act to challenge the other's presuppositions. It is like the life-term prisoners in the sick story who are so familiar with each other's jokes that it suffices to recount them by announcing their number. You begin to feel corseted in responding to *their* arguments or in noting settled agreements. The topic becomes interpersonally boring and, by unspoken mutual consent, it is either dropped or simply indicated by something like the life-termer's number.

Boredom is a powerful phenomenon—a poison to the intellectual in large doses. And like many poisons, it is a rather benign stimulant in small doses. I think it always infuses intellectual work in some deep way. For all of the sciences and most of the humane disciplines of learning proceed by working with the familiar and attempting to rearrange it in certain ways so as to make the familiar generate something novel. It is inevitable that, from time to time, we get trapped in the familiar and suffer its boredom. Dialogue with others provides some escape from the procrustean familiarity of our "subject." But, alas, dialogue eventually goes the route of the life-termer's story.

But just here the essay as a form comes into its own. It is an invitation to ignore the constraints of the other that you encounter in dialogue, to consider and to unpack any presupposition without giving umbrage and to do it in a manner that permits a use of metaphor forbidden to the logician or scientist. Yet the essay form is tightly wrought enough to keep one's nose not so much to the grindstone as to the touchstone. Indeed, David Olson insists (and I think with good reason) that it is characteristic of the essay form, and may even be its historical origin, to try to transcend the constraints of dialogue and its context-bound definitions of truth—"the meaning is in the text," as Luther urged.

I remarked that each of the essays in the volume grew out of an encounter with certain matters that had interested me. Obviously, they come out of a common source, and friends have said to me that it is a very personal book. That may well be because the topics were ones I could not cope with by the universalized methods of experiment or logical analysis alone. Hence the subtitle: "Essays for the Left Hand." The left hand, *my* left hand, has known hard times since these essays were published. Or perhaps it would be better to say, left hands in the sixties and seventies were otherwise occupied, and principally with the politics of the revolution through which we have been living.

There has been Vietnam, the student uprising, the emergence of a Third World, and the battle against racial and ethnic discrimination. It was impossible not to be involved. The clumsy cruelties of the student protests and the infamous "police bust" at Harvard in response drove me more deeply into an active role in the day-to-day life of the University. I became involved in school reform, in Africa, in Head Start. Were the times better suited for action than for reflection?

I recall sitting as chairman of the committee appointed by the president of Harvard to liquidate the Reserve Officers Training Corps at the university. Across the table were the representatives of the Navy and Army, serving officers with whom I disagreed but whom I greatly respected. I recall too, at the same time, the students and tutors in my Harvard house. I also admired their nerve and conviction in "trying on" new ideas and life styles. Though I didn't agree with them either, my respect for their integrity was complete. Perhaps I am the typical conflict-laden liberal, torn by an appreciation of contrary excellencies.

That period was a time for tracts rather than essays, particularly essays for the left hand. The essay form did not return my way for a decade, and then it emerged as the Herbert Spencer Lecture delivered at Oxford in 1976. It is the only new essay in this volume, and I am particularly pleased to have it included. It restored my faith in the importance of the essay as an intellectual experience.

In the seventeen years since the first publication of *On Knowing* there has been a steady polarization within psychology between the "hardnosed," psychonomic study of psychology and the more "humanistic," methodologically unconstrained approach. Those at the far reach of each movement have had a tendency to heap scorn on the other. Within the American Psychological Society, there are separate divisions where each lives, and the hardnosed genus of psychologist has set up a separate society—the Psychonomic Society. I see in both extremes a manifestation of anti-intellectualism: the one denigrating the processes that give rise to hypotheses, the other damning the techniques designed for their testing. I find myself uneasy with both extremes. My idea has always been that the antic activities of the left hand offer gifts to the right for closer scrutiny and hardnosed testing.

In Great Britain, psychology is not much liked. It is seen as an upstart discipline and one without either a settled body of theory or a method of work and, supreme sin, cut off from the more humane and literary approaches to the study of man. It has been the reaction of some British psychologists to become even more implacably positivistic in their approach and to cultivate a connection with either biology or the computational sciences. The tempering effect of the psychology of language that has done so much to keep American psychology from dividing totally into separate fields is not nearly so evident in Britain. "Psychology and the Image of Man" was my effort to bring the two views of psychology back into single focus. It did not convince many of my Oxford friends who were initially of a contrary view, but unpopular views may at least seem to raise consciousness about alternatives. In any case, it created a good row—and that is always welcome on the British intellectual scene!.

I don't think that psychology should enter the age-old battle to understand the nature of man with one hand tied behind its back—left *or* right. I can put it best in terms of a lament of a former postdoctoral fellow in my laboratory at Oxford—Michael Scaife who had just taken his degree in bird behavior and had been awarded a fellowship to be "retreaded" as a human psychologist. He said that when he worked on animal behavior he felt constantly deprived by the species difference between him and his subjects. He had always wanted to "get into their minds." Now that he was working on human beings he kept encountering critics who urged him to ignore the fact that he was the same species as his subjects. He had chosen to study how infants learned to share a common attentional focus with their mothers. How *could* he overlook what he already knew as a human being about shared attention! It is surely foolish to pretend that it makes no difference that we are human beings when we begin to study human beings. It is enormously useful to have, in their full subjectivity, works such as A. R. Luria's accounts of the mind of a mnemonist and of the shattered world of one of his brain-injured patients. They are rich in evocation, a seedbed of hypotheses. And they are, each in its way, bits of literary art.

I hope we can encourage our students to use their own knowledge of the human condition, of themselves or their language or their families to derive, if not a hypothesis, at least a hunch that will start them on their way toward one. It would be a pity if we psychologists were to be condemned to a one-handed existence. It is a curious though not really an immodest thing to say, but I found that the rereading of these essays—my *own* essays—lured me back into a reconsideration of the unfinished business that had started them into existence in the first place. Perhaps, with some unpredictable luck, they may lead others back to some unfinished business of their own.

                                                          J. S. B.

Wolfson College
Oxford
January 1979

Preface

There are many debts to acknowledge and credits to be given—to the friends with whom one dines, to the colleagues with whom one works, to the students whose impatience helps keep a sense of doubt well nourished, to those administering spirits who keep chaos from descending, to foundations that have made some free time possible. The existence of a great university also makes a deep difference. Josiah Royce, commenting on the Harvard community, once remarked that for it talking was the most natural form of breathing.

Several close friends have been particularly generous in advice and encouragement. George Miller, Albert Guerard, and Elting Morison have been sources of instruction and models of patience. Elizabeth Weems Solomon could be counted on for arresting advice. Mark Saxton has labored with me long and generously in the process of making a continuity of the ideas expressed in these essays. Ruth and Richard Tolman, whose loss many of us still feel, encouraged me long ago in the pursuits reported here. My wife, Blanche Marshall Bruner, has been a constant and illuminating companion in the making of the book.

Museums and photographers are credited in the text. The following publishers and periodicals have given generous permission to reproduce material: Faber & Faber, Ltd., George Braziller, Inc., *Harvard Educational Review, International Journal of Psychology*, The Macmillan Company, *The Mathematics Teacher, Partisan Review, Psychological Review, The Reporter*, Rupert Hart-Davis, Ltd., and *Saturday Review Education Supplement*.

Cambridge, Massachusetts   J. S. B.
January 1962

Contents

on
   Knowing

Introduction

You are concerned, let us say, with the nature of myth and wherein it plays a role in man's thinking. An occasion arises—perhaps an invitation to speak or to contribute an article to a magazine—and you commit your thoughts to paper. Some years later there is another occasion: this time the topic, presumably a different one, may be freedom and the control of behavior. Only later, only in retrospect, does a continuity emerge. In any man's intellectual life there are only a few topics, only a limited set of persistent queries and themes.

This book took its origin in a collection of occasion pieces, essays written for the left hand, as I shall explain in a moment. The intent was to bring them out one day much as they had originally been written. But as I worked over them, they changed and merged and were no longer so occasional. The period of five years over which they had been written melted and the underlying themes emerged in their own right.

The themes are few enough in number. The first part of the book concerns itself with how we construct reality by the process of knowing: it deals with the act of knowing in itself and how it is shaped and in turn gives form to language, science, literature, and art. In effect, we shall be dealing with the issue of how we know and how knowledge reflects the structuring power of the human intellect.

But one's conception of knowing and of the nature of what

is known perforce lead one to a concern with how we impart knowledge, how we teach, how we lead the learner to construct a reality on his own terms. The second part of the book entertains conjectures on the nature of teaching and learning, conjectures that grew, in spirit if not in original sequence, from issues raised earlier. But sequence is a fiction, and in a human life what follows may have produced what went before.

Finally, the last part of the book examines how one's conception of reality, affected as it is by the uncertainties of seeking to know, influences action and commitment.

Since childhood, I have been enchanted by the fact and the symbolism of the right hand and the left—the one the doer, the other the dreamer. The right is order and lawfulness, *le droit*. Its beauties are those of geometry and taut implication. Reaching for knowledge with the right hand is science. Yet to say only that much of science is to overlook one of its excitements, for the great hypotheses of science are gifts carried in the left hand.

Of the left hand we say that it is awkward and, while it has been proposed that art students can seduce their proper hand to more expressiveness by drawing first with the left, we nonetheless suspect this function. The French speak of the illegimate descendant as being *à main gauche*, and, though the heart is virtually at the center of the thoracic cavity, we listen for it on the left. Sentiment, intuition, bastardy. And should we say that reaching for knowledge with the left hand is art? Again it is not enough, for as surely as the recital of a daydream differs from the well-wrought tale, there is a barrier between undisciplined fantasy and art. To climb the barrier requires a right hand adept at technique and artifice.

And so I have argued in one of the essays in this volume that the scientist and the poet do not live at antipodes, and I urge in another that the artificial separation of the two modes of knowing cripples the contemporary intellectual as an effective mythmaker for his times. But it is not principally in the role of a would-be mediator between the humanist and the scientist that I have written and then rewritten the essays that comprise this book. My objective, rather, is somewhat different, perhaps more personal.

It is to explore the range of the left hand in dealing with the nature of knowing. As a right-handed psychologist, I have been diligent for fifteen years in the study of the cognitive processes: how we acquire, retain, and transform knowledge of the world in which each of us lives—a world in part "outside" us, in part "inside." The tools I have used have been those of the scientific psychologist studying perception, memory, learning, thinking, and (like a child of my times) I have addressed my inquiries to the laboratory rat as well as to human beings. At times, indeed, I have adopted the role of the clinician and carried out therapy with children whose principal symptom presented at the clinic was a "learning block," an inability to acquire knowledge in a formal school setting, though their intelligence seemed normal or even superior. More recently, I have turned my attention to the nature of the teaching process in an effort to formulate the outlines of a "theory of instruction" and so better to understand what we seek to do when we guide another's learning either by a lecture or by that formidable thing known as a curriculum. Seeking the most beautifully simple case, I chose to study the learning and teaching of mathematics. But it was soon clear that the heart of mathematical learning was tipped well to the left. There have been times when, somewhat discouraged by the complexities of the psychology of knowing, I have sought to escape through neurophysiology, to discover that the neurophysiologist can help only in the degree to which we can ask intelligent psychological questions of him.

One thing has become increasingly clear in pursuing the nature of knowing. It is that the conventional apparatus of the psychologist—both his instruments of investigation and the conceptual tools he uses in the interpretation of his data—leaves one approach unexplored. It is an approach whose medium of exchange seems to be the metaphor paid out by the left hand. It is a way that grows happy hunches and "lucky" guesses, that is stirred into connective activity by the poet and the necromancer looking sidewise rather than directly. Their hunches and intuitions generate a grammar of their own—searching out connections, suggesting similarities, weaving ideas loosely in a trial web. Once, having come in late to dine at King's College, Cambridge, with my friend Oliver Zangwill, I found myself seated next to a delightful older man whose name I had not caught in the hurried and mumbled introductions. We agreed that the climate of debate at Cambridge might be vastly improved if some far-sighted philanthropist would establish a chair of The Black Arts and Thaumaturgy, that the effort to know had become too aseptic and constrained. My neighbor at table turned out to be E. M. Forster.

The psychologist, for all his apartness, is governed by the same constraints that shape the behavior of those whom he studies. He too searches widely and metaphorically for his hunches. He reads novels, looks at and even paints pictures, is struck by the power of myth, observes his fellow men intuitively and with wonder. In doing so, he acts only part-time like a proper psychologist, racking up cases against the criteria derived from an hypothesis. Like his fellows, he observes the human scene with such sensibility as he can muster in the hope that his insight will be deepened. If he is lucky or if he has subtle psychological intuition, he will from time to time come up with hunches, combinatorial products of his metaphoric activity. If he is not fearful of these products of his own subjectivity, he will go so far as to tame the metaphors that have produced the hunches, tame them in the sense of shifting them from the left hand to the right hand by rendering them into notions that can be tested. It is my impression from ob-

serving myself and my colleagues that the forging of metaphoric hunch into testable hypothesis goes on all the time.
And I am inclined to think that this process is the more
evident in psychology where the theoretical apparatus is not
so well developed that it lends itself readily to generating
interesting hypotheses.

Yet because our profession is young and because we feel
insecure, we do not like to admit our humanity. We quite
properly seek a distinctiveness that sets us apart from all those
others who ponder about man and the human condition—all
of which is worthy, for thereby we forge an intellectual discipline. But we are not satisfied to forge distinctive methods
of our own. We must reject whoever has been successful in
the task of understanding man—if he is not one of us. We place
a restrictive covenant on our domain. Our articles, submitted
properly to the appropriate psychological journal, have about
them an aseptic quality designed to proclaim the intellectual
purity of our psychological enterprise. Perhaps this is well,
though it is not enough.

It is well, perhaps, because it is economical to report the
products of research and not the endless process that constitutes the research itself. But it is not enough in the deeper
sense that we may be concealing some of the most fruitful
sources of our ideas from one another. I have felt that the self-
imposed fetish of objectivity has kept us from developing a
needed genre of psychological writing—call it protopsychologi-
cal writing if you will—the preparatory intellectual and emotional labors on which our later, more formalized, efforts are
based. The genre in its very nature is literary and metaphoric,
yet it is something more than this. It inhabits a realm midway
between the humanities and the sciences. It is the left hand
trying to transmit to the right.

I find myself a little out of patience with the alleged split
between "the two cultures," for the two are not simply external
ways of life, one pursued by humanists, the other by scientists.

They are ways of living with one's own experience. I recall a painfully withdrawn young physicist at the Institute for Advanced Study when I was a visiting member of that remarkable institution. His accomplishments as a flutist were magical; he could talk and live either music or physics. For all the rightness of his life, it was nonetheless a segmented one. What was lacking was not an institutionalized cultural bridge outside, but an internal transfer from the left to the right—and perhaps there was one, though my colleague could not admit it. It is a little like the amusing dialogue Louis MacNeice reports between himself and W. H. Auden on their trip to Iceland:

> And the don in me set forth
> How the landscape of the north
> Had educed the saga style
> Plodding forward mile by mile.
> And the don in you replied
> That the North begins inside,
> Our ascetic guts require
> Breathers from the Latin fire.

But the left hand is not all. For there is also in these pages much about the profound revolution that has been taking place in the sciences of man during the past decade and of the new dilemmas that have replaced the old ones. We know now, for example, that the nervous system is not the one-way street we thought it was—carrying messages from the environment to the brain, there to be organized into representations of the world. Rather, the brain has a program that is its own, and monitoring orders are sent out from the brain to the sense organs and relay stations specifying priorities for different kinds of environmental messages. Selectivity is the rule and a nervous system, in Lord Adrian's phrase, is as much an editorial hierarchy as it is a system for carrying signals.

We have learned too that the "arts" of sensing and knowing consist in honoring our highly limited capacity for taking in and processing information. We honor that capacity by learning the methods of compacting vast ranges of experience in economical symbols—concepts, language, metaphor, myth, formulae. The price of failing at this art is either to be trapped in a confined world of experience or to be the victim of an overload of information. What a society does for its members, what they could surely not achieve on their own in a lifetime, is to equip them with ready means for entering a world of enormous potential complexity. It does all this by providing the means of simplification—most notably, a language and an ordering point of view to go with the language.

This has also been the decade in which the role of activity and environmental complexity has become clear to us—both in the maintenance of normal human functioning and in the development of human capacities. The isolation experiments have made it clear that an immobilized human being in a sensorially impoverished environment soon loses control of his mental functions. The daring and brilliant experiments inspired by Donald Hebb at McGill have shown the degree to which alertness depends on a constant regimen of dealing with environmental diversity. And as if this were not enough, we also know now that the early challenges of problems to be mastered, of stresses to be overcome, are the preconditions of attaining some measure of our full potentiality as human beings. The child is father to the man in a manner that may be irreversibly one-directional, for to make up for a bland impoverishment of experience early in life may be too great an obstacle for most organisms. Indeed, recent work indicates that for at least one species, the utilitarian rat, too much gray homogeneity in infancy may produce chemical changes in the brain that seem to be associated with dullness. One wonders, then, about the issue of the appropriate exercise of mind early in life as a condition for fullness later.[1]

Perhaps too, and for the first time, we have come to a sense

---

[1] For more details of this phase of work in psychology over the past decade, see Philip Solomon and others, eds., *Sensory Deprivation* (Cambridge: Harvard University Press, 1961).

of the nature of early mental life, indeed early intellectual life. My generation of psychologists has been fortunate in its exploration of early intellectual development—massively so in the flow of work that has come from Piaget at Geneva, and especially so in the quantitatively meager but brilliant work of the too-early dead Vygotsky at Moscow. Piaget has given us a respectful sense of the manner in which an intrinsic and self-contained logic characterizes mental operations at any stage of development, however primitive it may be. Vygotsky has given us a vision of the role of internalized dialogue as the basis of thought, a guarantor of social patterning in that most lonely sphere, the exercise of mind.

The decade in psychology and its allied fields has been energizing: the lock step of "learning theory" in this country has been broken, though it is still the standard village dance. It is apparent to many of us that the so-called associative connecting of physical stimuli and muscular responses cannot provide the major part of the explanation for how men learn to generate sentences never before spoken, or how they learn to obey the laws of the sonnet while producing lines never before imagined. Indeed, all behavior has its grammatical consistency; all of it has its consistency of style.

Perhaps the moment is uniquely propitious for the left hand, for a left hand that might tempt the right to draw freshly again, as in art school when the task is to find a means of imparting new life to a hand that has become too stiff with technique, too far from the scanning eye. In any case, the chapters that follow, mostly concerned with knowing and its significance, are written in that spirit.

PART I ◄

the Shape of Experience

I had been asked to study a highly productive invention group, attached to an industrial consulting firm of world-wide reputation. It was a curious group: though they worked on problems that might properly be called "engineering," the group contained no engineers. For a year, I sat in as a working member of this group, helping to design protective clothing for missile-loading teams that had to handle highly corrosive propellants. It was an illuminating experience in the sense that I discovered that I, with neither interest in nor knowledge of protective clothing or missiles or corrosives, could get deeply involved and, indeed, come up with some rather respectable ideas about how to get people into and out of protective suits. I even invented a technique for keeping the draft out of sleeping bags, a byproduct that properly ranks as beating swords into plowshares.

The effectiveness of the group members consisted in their sense of freedom to explore possibilities, in their devotion to elegant solutions, and in the interplay among them that, in effect, made each man stronger in the group than individually. During the year, I also had the benefit and pleasure of long discussion with two Cambridge friends, William J. J. Gordon and Jean MacKenzie Pool. The essay here, "The Conditions of Creativity," came out of my effort to bring together what I had observed and what I had seen and read before of creativity. There has been much work done in the field since 1959, when the piece was first written. Indeed, the work on the invention group has been admirably converted—through the analysis of tape recordings and statistical techniques—into a doctoral dis-

sertation at Radcliffe College, written by Dr. Betty Hosmer
Mawardi, now on the staff of Western Reserve University.

"The Conditions of Creativity," then, is a first attempt, a
preface to a more systematic analysis of creative invention. In
greatly modified form, it first saw the light of day at a symposium on creative thinking held at the University of Colorado
in the spring of 1959.

The next three essays in Part One were written in their first
form during 1959 and 1960. The circumstances that led me
to write them are all seemingly different. "Myth and Identity"
was prepared for a symposium held by the American Academy
of Arts and Sciences, a symposium since published in the pages
of *Daedalus* and then in *Myth and Mythmaking* (New York:
Brᵃziller, 1960). "Identity and the Modern Novel" was given
as a guest lecture in Albert Guerard's Harvard course on the
modern novel. Guerard and I had talked for years about giving
a joint course on the psychology of literature. We had spent
many evenings together discussing Gide, Conrad, Hardy, and
many younger novelists whose work he had led me to. An
exchange of guest lectures was as close as we came to realizing
our plan before he departed to take the chair in comparative
literature created in honor of his father at Stanford University.
The concluding section of the essay is based on a talk originally
prepared for the celebration of Radcliffe College's seventy-fifth
birthday. "Art as a Mode of Knowing" was written originally
as a long letter to a painter friend, Mrs. Izler Solomon, who
had been struggling bravely to teach me to paint and to look
more wisely at pictures. The letter was eventually converted
into a lecture for a course I was giving and finally into its
present form.

There is a circumstance that relates the three pieces to each
other. I was then studying learning blocks, the conditions that
prevent children from learning, from exercising their normal
curiosity. I had come upon the phenomenon of the "pre-

emptive metaphor" in that work: the technique by which many seemingly unrelated things are tied together by a common fear and a common avoidance. The joining of such disparate collections of fears seemed to be metaphoric. I was struck by the fact that metaphor, so often the vehicle for mythic leaping, could also be a device for a kind of cancerous illness. The cancerous quality was in the manner of the spread of a fear—akin to what in medicine is called metastasis, what in literary analysis is referred to as synecdoche. Let me illustrate from one of the cases then in treatment—a boy with a fatiguing load of pent-up hostility with the impossible, family-supported ideal of not expressing any of it. School learning had become extremely difficult for this fourteen-year-old; in his mind it had become associated with aggressive competition and rebellion within the confines of his family, literally a battle against a family image that cast boys and men in the role of intellectual ne'er-do-wells. The boy's father had accepted the role; indeed, it had been well established early when his then high-school sweetheart, his present wife, had helped him squeak through graduation. After that, the father had settled into a semiskilled job, perhaps somewhat uneasily, and the mother had taken on the mantle of family intellectual and doer of good works. An older sister had just finished high school with a strong record and was on her way through nurse's training.

The unconscious preoccupation of this boy was aggression and, when the preoccupation was aroused, he would freeze and, in his words, "turn stupid." Once rapport had been achieved between the boy and his therapist, it became clear how widely the fear had spread, what a range it had come to cover. In arithmetic, for example, he saw fractions as "cut-up numbers," and the operation of algebraic cancellation was "killing off numbers and letters on both sides of the equal sign." Graphing a simple arithmetic progression at one tutorial session, he was asked to guess where the line would go next, given several points already plotted. He said that when it got high enough up on the graph it would explode and come back down. Once he commented to his tutor that pencils were dangerous because of their sharp points which were like knives, and then went on to muse that any piece of wood could also be dangerous because you could sharpen it, and it was plain that he could have carried this pre-emptive metaphor further if he had not been interrupted by the demands of the tutorial.

I had read a piece by Mark Schorer on metaphor ("Fiction and the 'Matrix of Analogy,'" *Kenyon Review,* XI, 1949) and the fine book by Calvin Hall dealing with the metaphoric devices found in dreams (*The Meaning of Dreams,* New York: Harper, 1953). It struck me that the metaphoric device of the dream and the metaphoric device of the poet are the same but for one thing—that ineffable thing, the work of the artist. Yet it was also clear to me that some dreams are rich and beautiful, others impoverished and crude, that dream work and the work of art might also share a certain discipline. What is characteristic of the great work of art is that its metaphoric artifice, its juxtapositions, have not only surprise value but also illuminating honesty. The two combine to create what we shall later refer to as "effective surprise." The work of art also has a cognitive economy in its metaphoric transformations, which make it possible for a seemingly limited symbol to spread its power over a range of experience. Neurotic symbolism and the metaphors of dreaming are somehow cloudy or even opaque.

Perhaps the surprise of the metaphoric juxtaposition where illness intervenes is too honest for the patient to face, given his responses. The result is defense and denial, an avoidance of the disturbing honesty at all costs. There is "overanticipating" of what is likely to be internally dangerous; too many things are put on the danger list. In consequence, the neurotic steers clear of what he anticipates as dangerous and is unable to learn whether he can cope with them. The economy of the mechanism is that the defensiveness is too efficient. Like Henry James's protagonist in "The Beast in the Jungle," the neurotic avoids everything that *might* be dangerous and in the end is immobilized. It is this overefficient pre-emptiveness that makes such metaphoric activity sick, in contrast to the illuminating quality of great myth and great poetry.

All of these considerations led me to a concern with the positive side of metaphoric and literary thinking. What is the artifice that creates illumination rather than illness? The first essay explores myth itself and the manner in which life creates myth and then imitates it. The second essay treats some representative modern novels with a view to examining wherein the modern novel and the classic myth differ in their approach to metaphoric transformations of life. The last essay in the group concentrates on the devices of the painter and, when it is rewritten in some other guise some later day, it will show an even stronger stamp of the thinking of my friend Ernst Gombrich whose *Art and Illusion* is such a monumental achievement.

Our insights into mental functioning are too often fashioned from observations of the sick and the handicapped. It is difficult to catch and record, no less to understand, the swift flight of man's mind operating at its best.

The Conditions of Creativity

There is something antic about creating, although the enterprise be serious. And there is a matching antic spirit that goes with writing about it, for if ever there were a silent process it is the creative one. Antic and serious and silent. Yet there is good reason to inquire about creativity, a reason beyond practicality, for practicality is not a reason but a justification after the fact. The reason is the ancient search of the humanist for the excellence of man: the next creative act may bring man to a new dignity.

There is, alas, a shrillness to our contemporary concern with creativity. Man's search for the sources of dignity changes with the pattern of his times. In periods during which man saw himself in the image of God, the creation of works *ad majorem gloriam dei* could provide a sufficient rationale for the dignity of the artist, the artisan, the creative man. But in an age whose dominant value is a pragmatic one and whose massive achievement is an intricate technological order, it is not sufficient to be merely useful. For the servant can pattern himself on the master—and so he did when God was master and Man His servant creating works in His glory—but the machine is the servant of man, and to pattern one's function on the machine provides no measure for dignity. The machine is useful, the system in terms of which the machines gain their use is efficient, but what is man?

The artist, the writer, and to a new degree the scientist seek

an answer in the nature of their acts. They create or they
seek to create, and this in itself endows the process with
dignity. There is "creative" writing and "pure" science, each
justifying the work of its producer in its own right. It is
implied, I think, that the act of a man creating is the act of a
whole man, that it is this rather than the product that makes
it good and worthy. So whoever seeks to proclaim his wholeness turns to the new slogan. There is creative advertising,
creative engineering, creative problem solving—all lively
entries in the struggle for dignity in our time. We, as psychologists, are asked to explicate the process, to lay bare the essence
of the creative. Make no mistake about it: it is not simply as
technicians that we are being called, but as adjutants to the
moralist. My antic sense rises in self-defense. My advice, in
the midst of the seriousness, is to keep an eye out for the tinker
shuffle, the flying of kites, and kindred sources of surprised
amusement.

We had best begin with some minimum working definition
that will permit us at least to look at the same set of things.
An act that produces *effective surprise*—this I shall take as the
hallmark of a creative enterprise. The content of the surprise
can be as various as the enterprises in which men are engaged.
It may express itself in one's dealing with children, in making
love, in carrying on a business, in formulating physical theory,
in painting a picture. I could not care less about the person's
intention, whether or not he intended to create. The road to
banality is paved with creative intentions. Surprise is not easily
defined. It is the unexpected that strikes one with wonder or
astonishment. What is curious about effective surprise is that
it need not be rare or infrequent or bizarre and is often none
of these things. Effective surprises, and we shall spell the
matter out in a moment, seem rather to have the quality of
obviousness about them when they occur, producing a shock
of recognition following which there is no longer astonishment.
It is like this with great formulae, as in that for the conserva-

tion of energy or for the brilliant insight that makes chemistry possible, the conservation of mass. Weber's stunning insight into the nature of a just noticeable sensory difference is of this order, that before a difference will be noticed it must be a constant fraction of the sensory intensity presently being experienced: $\Delta I / I = K$.

I think it is possible to specify three kinds of effectiveness, three forms of self-evidence implicit in surprise of the kind we have been considering. The first is predictive effectiveness. It is the kind of surprise that yields high predictive value in its wake—as in the instance of the formula for falling bodies or in any good theoretical reformulation in science. You may well argue that predictive effectiveness does not always come through surprise, but through the slow accretion of knowledge and urge—like Newton with his *hypothesis non fingo*. I will reply by agreeing with you and specifying simply that whether it is the result of intuitive insight or of slow accretion, I will accept it within my definition. The surprise may only come when we look back and see whence we have come.

A second form of effectiveness is best called formal, and its most usual place is in mathematics and logic—possibly in music. One of the most beautiful descriptions of the phenomenon is to be found in G. H. Hardy's engaging A *Mathematician's Apology*. It consists of an ordering of elements in such a way that one sees relationships that were not evident before, groupings that were before not present, ways of putting things together not before within reach. Consistency or harmony or depth of relationship is the result. One of the most penetrating essays that has ever been written on the subject is, of course, Henri Poincaré's in his *Science and Method*. He speaks of making combinations that "reveal to us unsuspected kinship between . . . facts, long known, but wrongly believed to be strangers to one another."

Of the final form of effectiveness in surprise it is more difficult to write. I shall call it metaphoric effectiveness. It, too, is effective by connecting domains of experience that were before apart, but with the form of connectedness that has the discipline of art.

It is effective surprise that produces what Melville celebrated as the shock of recognition. Jung speaks of art that can produce such metaphoric connectedness as "visionary" in contrast to the merely psychological. It is, for example, Thomas Mann's achievement in bringing into a single compass the experiences of sickness and beauty, sexuality and restraint in his *Death in Venice*. Or it is the achievement of the French playwright Jean Anouilh who in *Antigone* makes Creon not only a tyrant but a reasonable man. What we are observing is the connecting of diverse experiences by the mediation of symbol and metaphor and image. Experience in literal terms is a categorizing, a placing in a syntax of concepts. Metaphoric combination leaps beyond systematic placement, explores connections that before were unsuspected.

I would propose that all of the forms of effective surprise grow out of combinatorial activity—a placing of things in new perspectives. But it is somehow not simply a taking of known elements and running them together by algorithm into a welter of permutations. One could design a computer to do that, but it would be with some embarrassment, for this is stupid even for a computer, and an ingenious computer programmer can show us much more interesting computer models than that. "To create consists precisely in not making useless combinations and in making those which are useful and which are only a small minority. Invention is discernment, choice." If not a brute algorithm, then it must be a heuristic that guides one to fruitful combinations. What is the heuristic? Poincaré goes on to urge that it is an emotional sensibility: "the feeling of mathematical beauty, of the harmony of numbers and forms, of geometric elegance." It is this that guides one in making combinations in mathematics. But it is surely not enough. One hears physicists speak of "physical intuition" as distinguishing the good theorist from the mere formalist, the mathematician. I suspect that in each empirical field there is developed in the creating scientist a kind of "intuitive familiarity," to use a term that L. J. Henderson was fond of, that gives him a sense of what combinations are likely to have predictive effectiveness and which are absurd. What precisely this kind of heuristic consists of is probably difficult to specify without reference to the nature of the field in question, which is not to say that the working models are utterly different in different areas of empirical endeavor, for there is obviously some generality, too.

It seems unlikely that the heuristic either of formal beauty or of intuitive familiarity could serve for the artist, the poet, and the playwright. What genius leads Faulkner to create and combine a Temple Drake and a Popeye in *Sanctuary?* How does Dostoevsky hit upon the particular combination of the Grand Inquisitor and the Christ figure in *The Brothers Karamazov?* What leads Picasso to include particular objects in a painting? Picasso says to Christian Zervos: "What a sad thing for a painter who loves blondes but denies himself the pleasure of putting them in his picture because they don't go well with the basket of fruit! What misery for a painter who detests apples to have to use them all the time because they harmonize with the tablecloth! I put in my pictures everything I like. So much the worse for the things—they have to get along with one another." [1] However maddening such a remark may be coming from a painter, it does point up the essentially emotive nature of the painter's work and his criteria for judging the fitness of combination. So Yeats may write:

> God guard me from those thoughts men think
> In the mind alone;
> He that sings a lasting song
> Thinks in a marrow-bone.

---

[1] "Conversation with Picasso," *Cahiers d'Art* (Paris), 1935. Translated by Brewster Ghiselin in *The Creative Process* (New York: Mentor Books, 1952), p. 56.

But marrow-bones are not really enough for lasting songs. For if it is true, as Picasso and many before have said, that "a picture lives only through him who looks at it," then the artist must speak to the human condition of the beholder if there is to be effective surprise. I, for one, find myself compelled to believe that there are certain deep sharings of plight among human beings that make possible the communication of the artist to the beholder, and, while I object to the paraphernalia that Jung proposes when he speaks of the collective unconscious, I understand why he feels impelled to proffer the idea. The artist—whatever his medium—must be close enough to these conditions in himself so that they may guide his choice among combinations, provide him with the genuine and protect him from the paste.

The triumph of effective surprise is that it takes one beyond common ways of experiencing the world. Or perhaps this is simply a restatement of what we have been meaning by effective surprise. If it is merely that, let me add only that it is in this sense that life most deeply imitates art or that nature imitates science. Creative products have this power of reordering experience and thought in their image. In science, the reordering is much the same from one beholder of a formula to another. In art, the imitation is in part self-imitation. It is the case too that the effective surprise of the creative man provides a new instrument for manipulating the world—physically as with the creation of the wheel or symbolically as with the creation of $e = mc^2$.

One final point about the combinatorial acts that produce effective surprise: they almost always succeed through the exercise of technique. Henry Moore, who is unusually articulate both as craftsman and artist, tells us that he was driven to the use of holes in his sculpture by the technical problem of giving a sense of three-dimensionality to solid forms—"the hole connects one side to the other, making it immediately more three-dimensional," a discovery made while fretting over the puzzle of how to avoid relief carving on brittle material like stone. Joseph Conrad and Ford Madox Ford sat before a scene trying to describe it to each other in the most economical terms possible. Katherine Anne Porter sat on a camp stool before a landscape trying to jot down everything before her—and finally decided that she could not train her memory that way. Technique, then, and how shall we combine it eventually with the doctrine of inspiration?

As soon as one turns to a consideration of the conditions of creativity, one is immediately met by paradox and antinomy. A "determinant" suggests itself, and in the next pulse its opposite is suggested. I shall honor these antinomies and what I have to say will, as a result, seem at times paradoxical.

Detachment and commitment. A willingness to divorce oneself from the obvious is surely a prerequisite for the fresh combinatorial act that produces effective surprise. There must be as a necessary, if not a sufficient, condition a detachment from the forms as they exist. There are so many ways in which this expresses itself in creative activity that one can scarcely enumerate them. Wallace Stevens, among many, has written of the alienation of the poet from society and reality, and the spirit of this alienation is caught in his searching poem, "Notes Towards a Supreme Fiction." It is in part a condition for exploring one's own individuality, in part a means of examining the possibilities of human connection. The University as an institution, protected within its walls, should and sometimes does provide a basis for detachment insofar as it recognizes the inviolate privacy of those who inhabit it. The preoccupation of the scholar, gating out all but what seems relevant to his theme—this too is a vehicle of detachment. The creative writer who takes his journey without maps or his voyage into the interior, whether in the subjective Africas of Graham Greene or Joseph Conrad or in the interior jungles of Henry James or Marcel Proust—again it is detachment.

But it is a detachment of commitment. For there is about it a caring, a deep need to understand something, to master a technique, to rerender a meaning. So while the poet, the mathematician, the scientist must each achieve detachment, they do it in the interest of commitment. And at one stroke they, the creative ones, are disengaged from that which exists conventionally and are engaged deeply in what they construct to replace it.

Passion and decorum. By *passion* I understand a willingness and ability to let one's impulses express themselves in one's life through one's work. I use it in the sense, "he has a passion for painting," or, "she has a passion for cooking." I do not wish to raise or explore the Bohemian dilemma—whether the condition for passion in work is its expression in other forms of life. I happen to believe that Freud's fixed quantity of libido (express it here and it must be withdrawn from there) is a kind of first-order nonsense. Passion, like discriminating taste, grows on its use. You more likely act yourself into feeling than feel yourself into action. In any case, it is true of the creative man that he is not indifferent to what he does, that he is moved to it. For the artist, if not for the scientist, there is a tapping of sources of imagery and symbolism that would otherwise not be available—as expressed in the beautiful refrain line of Rimbaud's *Les Illuminations:* "J'ai seul la clef de cette parade sauvage." As for the scientist and the scholar, it is perhaps the eighteenth-century French philosopher, Helvetius, who, in his *Treatise on Man,* has put it best: "A man without *passions* is incapable of that degree of attention to which a superior judgment is annexed: a superiority that is perhaps less the effect of an extraordinary effort than an habitual attention."

But again a paradox: it is not all urgent vitality. There is a decorum in creative activity: a love of form, an etiquette toward the object of our efforts, a respect for materials. Rimbaud's wild beasts in the end are caged. For all that *Lord Jim* is a turbulent book, with the full range of human impulse, its raw power is contained by the decorum of the dispassionate gentlemanly narrator, Marlow. Herakles of the myth was not a hairy ape expressing his mastery indiscriminately: his shrewd trickery is the decorum. The wild flood of ideas that mathematicians like Hardy have described: eventually they are expressed in the courtesy of equations.

So both are necessary and there must surely be a subtle matter of timing involved—when the impulse, when the taming.

Freedom to be dominated by the object. You begin to write a poem. Before long it, the poem, begins to develop metrical, stanzaic, symbolical requirements. You, as the writer of the poem, are serving it—it seems. Or you may be pursuing the task of building a formal model to represent the known properties of single nerve fibers and their synapses: soon the model takes over. Or we say of an experiment in midstream that *it* needs another control group really to clinch the effect. It is at this point that we get our creative second wind, at the point when the object takes over. I have asked about a dozen of my most creative and productive friends whether they knew what I meant as far as their own work was concerned. All of them replied with one or another form of sheepishness, most of them commenting that one usually did not talk about this kind of personal thing. "This is when you know you're in and—good or bad—the thing will compel you to finish it. In a long piece of work it can come and go several times." The one psychologist among my informants was reminded of the so-called Zeigarnik completion tendency, suggesting that when the watershed was reached the task then had a structure that began to require completeness.

There is something odd about the phenomenon. We externalize an object, a product of our thoughts, treat it as "out there." Freud remarked, commenting on projection, that human beings seem better able to deal with stimuli from the outside than from within. So it is with the externalizing of a creative work, permitting it to develop its own being, its own autonomy coming to serve *it*. It is as if *it* were easier to cope with there, as if this arrangement permitted the emergence of more unconscious impulse, more material not readily accessible.

There is still another possibility. Observing children in the process of learning mathematics, I have been struck repeatedly by the economical significance of a good mode of representing things to oneself. In group theory, for example, it is extraordinarily difficult to determine whether a set of transformations constitutes a closed group so that any combination of them can be expressed by a single one. The crutch provided by a matrix that gets all the combinations out of the head on to paper or the blackboard makes it possible to look at the group structure as a whole, to go beyond it to the task of seeing whether it has interesting properties and familiar isomorphs. Good representation, then, is a release from intellectual bondage.

I have used the expression "freedom to be dominated" by the object being created. It is a strange choice of words, and I should like to explain it. To be dominated by an object of one's own creation—perhaps its extreme is Pygmalion dominated by Galatea—is to be free of the defenses that keep us hidden from ourselves.

As the object takes over and demands to be completed "in its own terms," there is a new opportunity to express a style and an individuality. Likely as not, it is so partly because we are rid of the internal juggling of possibilities, because we have represented them "out there" where we can look at them, consider them. As one friend, a novelist and critic, put it, "If it doesn't take over and you are foolish enough to go on, what you end up with is contrived and alien."

Deferral and immediacy. There is an immediacy to creating anything, a sense of direction, an objective, a general idea, a feeling. Yet the immediacy is anything but a quick orgasm of completion. Completion is deferred. Let me quote at some length from the conversation of Christian Zervos with Picasso:

> With me a picture is a sum of destructions. I make a picture, and proceed to destroy it. But in the end nothing is lost; the red I have removed from one part shows up in another.
>
> It would be very interesting to record photographically, not the stages of a painting, but its metamorphoses.[2] One would see perhaps by what course a mind finds its way towards the crystallization of its dream. But what is really very curious is to see that the picture does not change basically, that the initial vision remains almost intact in spite of appearance. I see often a light and a dark, when I have put them in my picture, I do everything I can to "break them up," in adding a color that creates a counter effect. I perceive, when this work is photographed, that what I have introduced to correct my first vision has disappeared, and that after all the photographic image corresponds to my first vision, before the occurrence of the transformations brought about by my will.[3]

This is not to say that there is not the occasional good luck, the piece that comes off lickety-split and finished, the theory hit upon at first fire. If ever Georges Simenon is acclaimed a great writer—and that he is more than simply competent is plain—then we will say he brings it off in a gush, in a quantum of pure energy and with such intensity, Carvel Collins tells us, that he has developed the custom of getting clearance from his doctor before he flings himself into a new novel.

Having read a good many journals and diaries by writers, I have come to the tentative conclusion that the principal guard against precocious completion, in writing at least, is boredom. I have little doubt that the same protection avails the scientist. It is the boredom of conflict, knowing deep down what one wishes to say and knowing that one has not said it. One acts on the impulse to exploit an idea, to begin. One also acts on the impulse of boredom, to defer. Thus Virginia Woolf, trying to finish *Orlando* in February 1928: "Always, always, the last chapter slips out of my hands. One gets bored. One whips oneself up. I still hope for a fresh wind and don't very

[2] My colleague Professor George Miller is now engaged in doing just this.—J. S. B.
[3] *The Creative Process*, pp. 56–57.

much bother, except that I miss the fun that was so tremen-
dously lively all October, November, and December." [4]

The internal drama. There is within each person his own
cast of characters—an ascetic, and perhaps a glutton, a prig,
a frightened child, a little man, even an onlooker, sometimes
a Renaissance man. The great works of the theater are de-
compositions of such a cast, the rendering into external drama
of the internal one, the conversion of the internal cast into
dramatis personae. Freud, in his searching essay on "The Poet
and the Daydream," is most discerning about this device of
the playwright.[5] There have been times when writers have
come too close to their own personal cast in constructing a
play, and even so able a craftsman of the theater as Goethe
stumbled in his *Torquato Tasso*, an embarrassingly transparent
autobiographical piece about the conflict between Tasso the
poet and Antonio the politician. It is, perhaps, Pirandello
among modern playwrights who has most convincingly mastered the technique, although a younger Italian dramatist, Ugo
Betti, showed promise of carrying it further before his premature death a few years ago. In his brilliant *The Queen and
the Rebels*, Betti includes an unforgettable scene at the political frontier of a mythical fascist state, the frontier guards
searching a bus party for the fleeing queen. As the scene
progresses, it becomes patent that the queen is a spineless
nonentity; it is the prostitute in the party who emerges as the
queen.

As in the drama, so too a life can be described as a script,
constantly rewritten, guiding the unfolding internal drama.
It surely does not do to limit the drama to the stiff characters
of the Freudian morality play—the undaunted ego, the brutish
id, the censorious and punitive superego. Is the internal cast
a reflection of the identifications to which we have been com-

---

[4] *A Writer's Diary* (New York: Harcourt, Brace, 1953), p. 121.
[5] For a discussion of Freud's use of the same device in the development
of psychoanalysis, see the chapter on "Freud and the Image of Man."

mitted? I do not think it is as simple as that. It is a way of grouping our internal demands and there are idealized models over and beyond those with whom we have special identification—figures in myth, in life, in the comics, in history, creations of fantasy.

There are some scripts that are more interesting than others. In some, there is a pre-empting protagonist in the center of the stage, constantly proclaiming, save for those moments when there are screamed intrusions from offstage, at which point the declaimer apologizes by pointing out that the voices are not really in the play. In others there is a richness, an inevitability of relationship, a gripping and constant exchange —or perhaps one should call it "inchange." These are dramatic personalities, producers of surprise.

I would like to suggest that it is in the working out of conflict and coalition within the set of identities that compose the person that one finds the source of many of the richest and most surprising combinations. It is not merely the artist and the writer, but the inventor too who is the beneficiary.

The dilemma of abilities. We have now looked at some of the paradoxical conditions that one might assume would affect the production of effective surprises—creativity. Nothing has been said about ability, or abilities. What shall we say of energy, of combinatorial zest, of intelligence, of alertness, of perseverance? I shall say nothing about them. They are obviously important but, from a deeper point of view, they are also trivial. For at any level of energy or intelligence there can be more or less of creating in our sense. Stupid people create for each other as well as benefiting from what comes from afar. So too do slothful and torpid people. I have been speaking of creativity, not of genius.

The chapter in Henry Adams' *Education*, "The Dynamo and the Virgin," is urbane, but beneath the urbanity there is a deep perplexity about what moves men, what moves history, what makes art. Adams spent the summer and fall of 1900 haunting the Great Exposition in Paris, particularly the hall of dynamos, until the dynamos "became a symbol of infinity . . . a moral force, much as the early Christians felt the Cross." During the same summer he made excursions to Notre Dame of Amiens and to Chartres, and it was then that he came to realize that the Virgin as symbol was also a source of energy: "All the steam in the world could not, like the Virgin, build Chartres." I end with the same perplexity in attempting to find some way of thinking reasonably about the creative process. At the outset I proposed that we define the creative act as effective surprise—the production of novelty. It is reasonable to suppose that we will someday devise a proper scientific theory capable of understanding and predicting such acts. Perhaps we will understand the energies that produce the creative act much as we have come to understand how the dynamo produces its energy. It may be, however, that there is another mode of approach to knowing how the process generates itself, and this will be the way in which we understand how symbols and ideas like the Virgin capture men's thoughts. Often it is the poet who grasps these matters most firmly and communicates them most concisely. Perhaps it is our conceit that there is only one way of understanding a phenomenon. I have argued that just as there is predictive effectiveness, so is there metaphoric effectiveness. For the while, at least, we can do worse than to live with a metaphoric understanding of creativity.

Myth and Identity

We know now a new origin of the faint hissing of the sea in the conch shell held to the ear. It is in part the tremor and throb of the hand, resonating in the shell's chambers. Yet, inescapably, it is the distant sea. For Yeats, it would have been a reaffirmation of his proper query:

O body swayed to music, O brightening glance,
How can we know the dancer from the dance?

And so with myth. It is at once an external reality and the resonance of the internal vicissitudes of man. Richard Chase's somewhat cumbersome definition will at least get us on our way: "Myth is an esthetic device for bringing the imaginary but powerful world of preternatural forces into a manageable collaboration with the objective (i.e., experienced) facts of life in such a way as to excite a sense of reality amenable to both the unconscious passions and the conscious mind." [1]

That myth has such a function—to effect some manner of harmony between the literalities of experience and the night impulses of life—few would deny. Yet I would urge that we not be too easily tempted into thinking that there is an oppositional contrast between *logos* and *mythos*, the grammar of experience and the grammar of myth. For each complements the other, and it is in the light of this complementarity that I wish to examine the relation of myth and personality.

[1] *Quest for Myth* (Baton Rouge: Louisiana State University Press, 1949).

Consider the myth first as projection, to use the conventional psychoanalytic term. I would prefer the term "externalization" better to make clear that we are dealing here with the process mentioned earlier in connection with works of art, scientific theories, inventions in general—the human preference to cope with events that are outside rather than inside. Myth, insofar as it is fitting, provides a ready-made means of externalizing human plight by embodying and representing them in storied plot and characters.

What is the significance of this externalizing tendency in myth? It is threefold, I would say. It provides, in the first instance, a basis for communion among men. What is "out there" can be named and shared in a manner beyond the sharing of subjectivity. By the subjectifying of our worlds through externalization, we are able, paradoxically enough, to share communally in the nature of internal experience. By externalizing cause and effect, for example, we may construct a common matrix of determinism. Fate, the full of the moon, the aether—these and not our unique fears are what join us in common reaction. Perhaps more important still, externalization makes possible the containment of terror and impulse by the decorum of art and symbolism. Given man's search for art forms, it must surely be no accident that there is no art of internal feeling or impulse. We seem unable to impose what Freud once called the artifice of formal beauty upon our internal sensations or even upon our stream of seemingly un-controlled fantasy. It is in the fact of fashioning an external product out of our internal impulses that the work of art begins. There is no art of kinesthesis, and, mindful of Aldous Huxley's fantasies, it is doubtful whether the titillation of the "feelies" could ever become an art form. Sharing, then, and the containment of impulse in beauty—these are the possi-bilities offered by externalization.

Of the economy provided by the externalized myth, little

need be said. Dollard and Miller, looking at the psychothera-
peutic process, have commented upon the importance of sort-
ing and "labeling" for the patient.[2] That is to say, if one is to
contain the panicking spread of anxiety, one must be able to
identify and put a comprehensible label upon one's feelings
better to treat them again, better to learn from experience.
Free-floating anxiety, as Freud's translators have vividly called
the internal terror that seem causeless to the sufferer, cries
for anchoring. Therapy, with its drawn-out "working through,"
provides an occasion for fashioning an anchor of one's own. So
too with hope and aspiring. In boundless form, they are pro-
logues to disenchantment. In time and as one comes to benefit
from experience, one learns that things will turn out neither
as well as one hoped nor as badly as one feared. Limits are set.
Myth, perhaps, serves in place of or as a filter for experience.
In the first of the world wars, the myth of the fearless soldier
forced a repression of the fear one felt in battle. The result,
often enough, was the dissociation and fugue of shell-shock.
A quarter century later, a second world war, governed by a
different concept of mythic human drama, had provided a
means of containment through the admission of human fear.
The case books of the two wars are as different as the myths
that men use to contain their fears and fatigue. The economical
function of myth is to represent in livable form the structure
of the complexities through which we must find our way. But
such representation, if it is to be effective, must honor the
canons of economy that make art.

Let me illustrate my point by reference to Homer, particularly to the madness of Ajax in the *Iliad*. Recall the occasion
of the death of Achilles and the determination of Thetis that
the bravest man before Ilium shall have her slain son's
arms. Agamemnon must make the fateful decision, and it is

[2] J. Dollard and N. E. Miller, *Personality and Psychotherapy* (New
York: McGraw-Hill, 1950).

Odysseus and not Ajax who receives the gift of Hephaestus-forged armor. Ajax is lashed by human anger and a craving for vengeance in a proportion to match his heroic capacities. But before these impulses can be expressed, there is an intervention by Athene: Ajax is struck mad and slaughters the captive Trojan livestock, cursing Agamemnon, Odysseus, and Menelaus the while, in a manner that would be described today as a massive displacement of aggression. It is Athene, then, who saves Ajax from a more direct expression of his fury and saves the Greeks from a slaughter of their leaders. Again we have the ingenious and rational intervention of the gods, a formal working out of internal plight in a tightly woven and dramatic plot. It is much as E. R. Dodds has suggested in examining the containment of irrationality in Greek myth. The clouding and bewildering of judgment that is *ate*, or the seemingly unnatural access of courage that is *menos*—both of these sources of potential disruption of natural order are attributed to an external agency, to a supernatural intervention, whether of the gods or of the Erinys.

I suggest that in general the inward monition, or the sudden unaccountable feeling of power, or the sudden unaccountable loss of judgment, is the germ out of which the divine machinery developed. One result of transposing the event from the interior to the external world is that the vagueness is eliminated: the indeterminate daemon has to be made concrete as some particular personal god.[3]

These were the gods that the Greeks shared, by virtue of whom a sense of causation became communal, through the nurturing of whom an art form emerged. The alternative, as Philip Rahv comments in discussing the governess in "The Turn of the Screw" and the chief protagonist in "The Beast in the Jungle," [4] is to give up one's allotment of experience. If one cannot externalize the demon where it can be enmeshed in the

[3] *The Greeks and the Irrational* (Boston: Beacon Press, 1957), pp. 14–15.
[4] *The Great Short Novels of Henry James* (New York: Dial Press, 1944), introduction.

texture of aesthetic experience, then the last resort is to freeze
and block: the overrepression and denial treated so perceptive-
ly by Freud in *The Problem of Anxiety.*

What is the art form of the myth? Principally it is drama;
yet for all its concern with preternatural forces and characters,
it is realistic drama that, in the phrase of Wellek and Warren,
tells of "origins and destinies." As they put it, it comprises "the
explanations a society offers its young of why the world is and
why we do as we do, its pedagogic images of the nature and
destiny of man." [5] Ernst Cassirer senses a proper antinomy
when he notes that the myth somehow emphasizes the facelike
character of experience while at the same time it has the
property of compelling belief. Its power is that it lives on the
feather line between fantasy and reality. It must be neither too
good nor too bad to be true, nor may it be too true. And if it
is the case that knowing through art has the function of connecting through metaphor what before had no apparent kinship, then in the present case the art form of the myth connects
the daemonic world of impulse with the world of reason by a
verisimilitude that conforms to each.

But there is a paradox. On the one side we speak of myth
as an externalization; on the other we speak of it as a pedagogic
image. This is surely a strange source of instruction! But it is
precisely here that the dramatic form of myth becomes sig-
nificant, precisely here where Gilbert Murray perceived the
genius of Homer and the Greeks: "This power of entering
vividly into the feelings of both parties in a conflict is . . . the
characteristic gift." [6]

I revert for a moment to a consideration of the human
personality, to the nature of the vicissitudes that are externalized in myth. It is far from clear why our discordant impulses
are bound and ordered in a set of identities—why one pattern

[5] René Wellek and Austin Warren, *Theory of Literature* (New York:
Harcourt, Brace, 1942), p. 180.
[6] *The Literature of Ancient Greece* (Chicago: University of Chicago
Press, 1957), p. 43.

of impulse is the self-pitying little man in us, another the nurturing protector, another the voice of moral indignation. Surely it is something more than the sum of identifications we have undertaken in the course of achieving balances between love and independence, coming to terms with those who have touched our lives. It is here that myth becomes the tutor, the shaper of identities; it is here that personality imitates myth in as deep a sense as myth is an externalization of the vicissitudes of personality.

Joseph Campbell writes:

In his life-form the individual is necessarily only a fraction and distortion of the total image of man. He is limited either as male or as female; at any given period of his life he is again limited as child, youth, mature adult, or ancient; furthermore, in his life-role he is necessarily specialized as craftsman, tradesman, servant, or thief, priest, leader, wife, nun, or harlot; he cannot be all. Hence the totality—the fullness of man—is not in the separate member, but in the body of the society as a whole; the individual can be only an organ.[7]

But if no man is all, there is at least in what Campbell calls the "mythologically instructed community" a corpus of images and identities and models that provides the pattern to which growth may aspire—a range of metaphoric identities. We are accustomed to speaking of myth in this programmatic sense in reference to history, as when Sorel invokes the general strike of all workers as a dynamic image, or when Christians speak of the Second Coming for which men must prepare themselves. In the same sense, one may speak of the corpus of myth as providing a set of possible identities for the individual personality. It would perhaps be more appropriate to say that the mythologically instructed community provides its members with a library of scripts upon which the individual may judge the play of his multiple identities. For myth, as I shall now try to illustrate, serves not only as a pattern to which one aspires but also as a criterion for the self-critic.

[7] *The Hero with a Thousand Faces* (New York: Meridian Books, 1956), pp. 382–383.

Take as an example the myths that embody and personify man's capacity for happiness. They are not infinite in variety, but varied enough. An early version is the Greek conception of the Five Ages of Man, the first of which is the happy Age of Gold. As Robert Graves tells it: "These men were the so-called golden race, subjects of Cronus, who lived without cares or labor, eating only acorns, wild fruit, and honey that dripped from the trees . . . never growing old, dancing, and laughing much; death to them was no more terrible than sleep. They are all gone now, but their spirits survive as happy genii." [8] This is the myth of happiness as innocence, and in the Christian tradition we know it as Man before the Fall. Innocence ends either by a successful attempt to steal the knowledge of God or by aspiring to the cognitive power of the gods, *hubris*. And with the end of innocence, there is an end to happiness; knowledge is equated with temptation to evil. The issue appears to revolve around the acquisition and uses of knowledge.

I will oversimplify in the interest of brevity and say that from these early myths there emerge two types of mythic plot: the plot of innocence and the plot of cleverness—the former being a kind of Arcadian ideal, requiring the eschewal of complexity and awareness, the latter requiring the cultivation of competence almost to the point of guile. The happy childhood, the good man as the child of God, the simple plowman, the Rousseauian ideal of natural nobility—these are the creatures of the plot of innocence. At the other extreme there are Penelope, the suitors, and Odysseus. In Murray's words:

Penelope—she has just learned on good evidence that Odysseus is alive and will return immediately—suddenly determines that she cannot put off the suitors any longer, but brings down her husband's bow, and says she will forthwith marry the man who can shoot through twelve axeheads with it! Odysseus hears her and is pleased! May it not be that in the original story there was a reason for Penelope to bring the bow, and for Odysseus to be pleased? It was a plot. He [Odysseus] meant Eurycleia [the old maidservant] to

[8] *The Greek Myths* (Baltimore: Penguin Books, 1955), p. 36.

recognize him [by his scar], to send the maids away, and break the news to Penelope. Then husband and wife together arranged the trial of the bow.[9]

Again and again in the Greek myths there are cleverness, competence, and artifice—Herakles, Achilles, Odysseus, Perseus —wherever you look. It is the happy triumph of clever competence with a supernatural assist. And yet there is also the ideal of the Age of Innocence. So too in the later Christian tradition and in our own times. The manner in which superior knowledge shows itself changes: the ideal of the crafty warrior, the wise man, the interpreter of the word of God, the Renaissance omnicompetent, the wily merchant, the financial wizard, the political genius. If it is true that in some way each is suspect, it is also true that each is idealized in his own way. Each is presented as satisfied. New versions arise to reflect the ritual and practice of each era—the modifications of the happiness of innocence and the satisfaction of competence.

The manner in which man has striven for competence and longed for innocence has reflected the controlling myths of the community. The medieval scholar, the Florentine prince, the guild craftsman, as well as the withdrawn monastic of Thomas à Kempis and the mendicant of St. Francis—all of these are deeply involved with the myths of innocence and competence and are formed by them. Indeed, the uncertainty in resolving the dichotomy of reason and revelation as ways to know God reflects the duality of the myth of happiness and salvation. It is not simply society that patterns itself on the idealizing myths, but unconsciously it is the individual man as well who is able to bring order to his internal clamor of identities in terms of prevailing myth. Life, then, produces myth and finally imitates it.

In our own time, in the American culture, there is a deep problem generated by the confusion that has befallen the myth of the happy man. It reflects itself in the American

[9] *The Literature of Ancient Greece,* pp. 39–40.

personality. There still lingers the innocent Christian conception that happiness is the natural state of man—or at least of the child and of man as innocent—and that it is something that we have done or failed to do as individuals that creates a rather Protestantized and private unhappiness. The impact of Freud has begun to destroy this myth, to replace it. Our popular films may now, with artistry, depict the child as murderer. A generation of playwrights has destroyed the remnants of Horatio Alger, replacing it with the image of Arthur Miller's salesman dying by entropy, an object of compassion. We are no longer a "mythologically instructed community." And so one finds a new generation struggling to find or to create a satisfactory and challenging mythic image.

Two such images seem to be emerging in the new generation. One is that of the hipsters and the squares; the other is the idealization of creative wholeness. The first is the myth of the uncommitted wandering hero, capable of the hour's subjectivity—its "kicks"—participating in a new inwardness. It is the theme of reduction to the essentially personal, the hero able to filter out the clamors of an outside world, an almost masturbatory ideal. Eugene Burdick in *The Reporter* gives the following account of a conversation in a San Francisco café between two members of the Beat Generation:

"Man, I remember something when I was little, a boy," somebody named Lee says. He is hunched forward, his elbows on the table, a tumbler of wine between his hands. "About a dog. Little miserable dog of mine."

"Yeah, man, go on," Mike says, his eyes lighting up.

"I get up real early to do my paper route. Los Angeles *Examiner*," Lee says. "Streets always empty, just a few milk trucks and bakery trucks and other kids like me. My dog goes along, see? Every day he trots along with me. Little mongrel dog."

"Yeah, yeah, go on, man," Mike says, impatient for the story, sure that it has meaning.

"There we are in all those big empty streets. Just me and the dog. Sun coming up, papers falling on the porches, me dreaming and walking and the dog trotting," Lee says. "Then far away, about as big as a black mosquito, I see this hopped-up Model A. Wonderful pipes on it, blatting so sweet I could hear them for six blocks. I stand there on the curb, listening to that sweet sound and watching that car come weaving down that empty street. And the dog stands in the gutter, watching too. That Model A gets bigger and I can see the chrome pipes on the side, the twin Strombergs sucking air, just eating up the asphalt."

He pauses and Mike leans forward and says urgently, "Now man, come on, go. I wanna hear this."

"This Model A is a roadster and there is a Mexican driving and his girl with him," Lee says slowly, stalking the climax. "It weaves across the street, and me and the dog stare at it. And it comes for us in a big slow curve and hit that dog. His back broke in mid-air and he was dead when he hit the street again. Like a big man cracking a seed in his teeth . . . same sound, I mean. And the girl stare back at me and laughs. And I laugh. You see why, man?"

The two of them sit quietly, looking down at the wine and listening to the jazz. Mike glances once at Lee and then back at his glass. He has learned something secret and private about Lee, and that is good enough. After a while they sit back, smiling, and listen to the jazz.[10]

It is not easy to create a myth and to emulate it at the same time. James Dean and Jack Kerouac, Kingsley Amis and John Osborne, the Teddy Boys and the hipsters: they do not make a mythological community. They represent mythmaking in process as surely as Hemingway's characters or Scott Fitzgerald's. What is ultimately clear is that even the attempted myth must be a model for imitating, a drama to be tried on for fit. One sees the identities of a group of young men being "packaged" in terms of the unbaked myth. It is a mold, a prescription of characters, a plot. Whether the myth will be viable, whether it will fit the internal plight, we do not know. There are temporary myths, too. There was a myth of the supernatural birth of a dead woman's son, a myth Boas found in 1888 and again in 1900. By 1931 there was no trace of it.

What of the renewal of the myth of the full creative man? It is even more inchoate than the first, yet perhaps more

[10] "The Innocent Nihilists Adrift in Squaresville," *The Reporter*, 3 April 1958, p. 33.

important. It is, as we have seen in another context, the middle-aged executive sent back to the university by the company for a year, wanting humanities and not sales engineering; it is this man telling you that he would rather take life classes Saturday morning at the museum school than be president of the company; it is the adjectival extravaganza of the word "creative," as in "creative advertising." It is as if, given the demise of the myths of creation and their replacement by a scientific cosmogony that for all its formal beauty lacks metaphoric force, the theme of creating becomes internalized, creating anguish rather than, as in the externalized myths, providing a basis for psychic relief and sharing. Yet this self-contained image of creativity becomes, I think, the basis for a myth of happiness. But perhaps between the death of one myth and the birth of its replacement there must be a reinternalization, even to the point of a *culte de moi.* That we cannot yet know. All that is certain is that we live in a period of mythic confusion that may provide the occasion for a new growth of myth, myth more suitable for our times.

Indeed, one may ask whether the rise of the novel as an art form, and particularly the subjectification of the novel since the middle of the nineteenth century, whether these do not symbolize the voyage into the interior that comes with the failure of prevailing myths to provide external models toward which one may aspire. For when the prevailing myths fail to fit the varieties of man's plight, frustration expresses itself first in mythoclasm and then in the lonely search for internal identity. The novels of Conrad, of Hardy, of Gide, of Camus— paradoxically enough—provide man with guides for the internal search. One of Graham Greene's most tormented books, an autobiographical fragment on an African voyage, is entitled *Journey Without Maps.* Perhaps the modern novel, in contrast to the myth, is the response to the internal anguish that can find no external constraint in myth, a form of internal map.

But this is a matter requiring a closer scrutiny than we can give it here. Suffice it to say that the alternative to externalization in myth appears to be the internalization of the personal novel, the first a communal effort, the second the lone search for identity.

Identity and the Modern Novel

 History has been described, probably too simply, as man's effort to make a home for himself in the world. It might better be described as an extension of those urges that impel man to find antecedents for his acts and his dilemmas, to find a prologue for his posture toward the future. The writing of history and the quest for identity share a paradox. A society's grasp of its history and a man's sense of his identity, when fully achieved, are final acts. But a community washed by the currents of growth does not easily come to a sharing of its conception of origins or the meaning of events. And no man answers easily the questions: "Who am I, where do I belong, and of what am I capable?"

Why are such issues so elusive? Perhaps it is as a brilliantly intuitive woman once put it in trying to understand the James-Lange theory of emotion: "Yes, yes, what William James must have begun with is, 'How do I know what I am until I feel what I do?'" Marlow voyages up the Congo toward Kurtz in "Heart of Darkness" and is in a constant anguish of action. Conrad's "The Secret Sharer" is no conversation piece between the young captain and his double, Leggatt. At the climax, the captain takes his ship—"on my conscience it had to be thus close"—to a point where "the black mass of Koh-ring, like the gate of the everlasting night, towered over the taffrail." The alienated narrator in Camus' *The Stranger* achieves a sense of his identity only by living out the consequences of a senseless murder. It is not by accident that highly subjective novels are often mistaken for tales of adventure.

But surely the puzzle is deeper than the idea that identity inheres in action and that it is only through retrospection upon action that we find it. Whose action? Here, I think, lies the deeper puzzle to which the novelist addresses himself: the puzzle of retroflective knowledge about self and identity, the epistemologically impossible question, "who am I?" to which the philosopher Morris Cohen once replied, "and who is asking the question?" For there are many selves in a character, and their relation to each other is the matter that is often most obscure.

What complicates the search, then, is not the simple fact that identity inheres in action and must be sought there, but rather that the action is not single in its purpose. Once again we are looking for a cast, for a script, and for an *explication du texte*. This is why action is required, both in the novel and in life itself, why it is so difficult to know who you are until you feel what you do, what each "you" does. And that is not all—we must complicate the matter one degree further. It is Jung who has most strongly urged the complementary principle of human character: a function that is exercised has the effect of strengthening an opposite function. After a while the introvert develops strong extraversive needs; the man whose life has been governed exclusively by thinking craves in time the guide of feeling; the literal man searches eventually for ways of intuiting. So with the principal actors within the human character. Their rebellious understudies, if I may so designate them, are often of opposite persuasion, Jung's *Gegentypus*. Here is the origin of the "secret sharer" and "the double," here the core of what is so movingly funny about Walter Mitty.

The more intensely a life is lived, the more complete its singleness of purpose, the more compelling is the secret sharer. The more externally successful a life is, the more difficult it usually becomes to admit the contrary double into the play that governs the life.

Character and the company of identities that constitute it seem to emerge at times of crisis in the life of man. Crises have a certain chronology and, while they differ in depth and content in each life, there are certain constants. I should like to consider four works of fiction—Camus' *The Stranger*, Fitzgerald's *The Great Gatsby*, Conrad's "The Secret Sharer," and a little-known novel of Jules Romain called *The Death of a Nobody*. But I cannot do so before sketching some of the more universal forms crisis takes when it creates characters. I am grateful to Erik Erikson for his searching examination of these matters, and I shall lean heavily upon his conception of identity crises in what follows.[1]

The first of the crises, first in the sense that it is likely to be the one that occurs earliest in the life of man, surrounds the issue of trust and mistrust in the meaningfulness of life and of one's own actions. Its pattern lies in the intensive relation between mother and infant when consistency of love and support is demonstrated by the mother's ability and willingness to give succor and warmth and rightness to the infant's life, to respond to the child's actions in a manner that lends meaning and predictability to them. In Camus' *The Stranger*, failure to achieve such a sense of meaning results in Meursault's sense of absurdity, his lack of caring whether he marries Marie or whether his firm sends him to Paris—nothing much matters. He is in the grownup world of the man who has come to expect nothing but capriciousness and meaninglessness—first from his mother, then from life itself. It is a stroke of art on Camus' part that the novel should begin with the death of such a mother, and that the issue of guilt in Meursault's trial

[1] Erik H. Erikson, *Childhood and Society* (New York: W. W. Norton, 1950).

should rest so heavily on his failure to cry at her funeral, his smoking at the death vigil, his acceptance of *café au lait* from the warder. For him, no action is appropriate, none inappropriate: neither going to a Fernandel film, sleeping with Marie the day after the funeral, nor the pointless shooting of the Arab. It is in a paroxysm of rage against the priest's insistence on meaningfulness in life and death that he finally achieves the primitive identity that comes from wanting to live: "It was as if that great rush of anger had washed me clean, had emptied me of hope, and gazing up at the dark sky spangled with its signs and stars, for the first time, the first, I laid my heart open to the benign indifference of the universe." At last a defense against meaninglessness, the strongest defense: none at all. At last identity in an absurd world.

The second crisis occurs in its earliest form when personal autonomy becomes the issue, and it involves the problem of creating a line of demarcation between oneself and the pressures and influences of the outside world. This is the stage of life in which the child exerts his negativism in the interest of his positive identity—to be free, if only by negation. It is at this moment in growth that the personal pronoun becomes a repetitive feature of the child's vocabulary, as if "I" and "me" were verbal probes for exploring the outer bounds of his living space. Like the crisis of trust, this one also is never finished; it recurs in later versions in richer contexts. Where failure to resolve the crisis of trust leads to doomed struggles with the sense of absurdity, failure here introduces the theme of "touch-me-not": one holds back, or strikes out compulsively, or is shamed by the power others have over one.

At this point, the range of crises begins to extend beyond the nucleus of family. The first one of this order involves initiative, the power to explore, to feel one's way, to take the initiative in action. Failure this time leads to a gnawing sense of guilt, of doubt in action. As school becomes increasingly important, there is the struggle to avoid a sense of inferiority and mediocrity, to be able to exercise one's industry and competence, to make the initiative come to something that fits into a broader society. And on the heels of this another crisis is soon generated: concentration or diffuseness, the adolescent's struggle, continued in altered form through life, between a sense of one's own identity and the wish to be engaged, to belong, and to play many roles. This crisis bedevils the American, particularly the successful American—specters like Sinclair Lewis' Arrowsmith or Arthur Miller's Salesman. It is one of Gatsby's deep confusions, deeper perhaps than the dream of perpetual youth symbolized by Daisy.

With the end of adolescence there is the first crisis of adult love: intimacy or isolation. The popularity and flirtatiousness of the girl must be replaced by the fidelity and intimate sympathy of the woman; the exploitative, sentimental date mongering of the teen-age boy must change into the protective giving and receiving of love by the man. The countless false roads to intimacy and mutual sexuality between man and woman provide a never-ending source of themes. Promiscuity, violence, and the sinuous maneuvers whereby men attempt to turn their women into mothers to recapture an earlier and safer version of intimacy are among the means by which man isolates himself from intimacy.

Finally, there are the two typical crises of the middle years. In one man faces the possibility that he will either create or stagnate. In the other he sums up the personal balance, looking for integrity and fearing to find despair.

The crisis of creating comes at the moment when a man looks beyond his own life to a next generation—through his children, through his works. There is the emergence of a new responsibility. If the awareness of this new responsibility does not emerge, a man is beset by a sense of sterility. This essentially is the theme of Lorca's *Yerma*, an embittering crisis of childlessness.

The Spanish writer Calderón has put the meaning of integrity best. He calls it the conviction of the moral paternity of one's own soul. With this relationship accepted, one can understand how to follow and to lead, how to aid and be aided. But now when the search fails, there is despair and time seems too short to explore other roads. It is cruel to die and cruel to live. I suspect this is the crisis that impels the novelists whose works we shall examine now.

Of Conrad's "The Secret Sharer" much has already been written about its bearing on the sense of self. The young captain on his first command is standing the anchor watch. In the dark water there appears a swimmer, Leggatt. He is the fleeing mate of a vessel anchored in the same roadstead a few miles off. The mate comes aboard on the Jacob's ladder that has been inadvertently left over the side. He has escaped from irons on his own ship, the *Sephora*, where sometime earlier he had strangled a crew member; part of a heroic episode in which Leggatt had set a foresail that saved the ship from foundering in a wild sea. The captain hears out Leggatt's story, the tale of a competent but impulsive man. He hides him carefully in his own cabin, tortured by guilt and misgiving with the deceits that are required. Finally, the captain brings his ship perilously close to the shore to let Leggatt escape, having given him a hat and some coins. The puzzle is why he did hide Leggatt, an outlaw, and, having hid him, why he brought his own ship so dangerously close in on shore when Leggatt had obviously been able to swim a few miles to get from the *Sephora* to the foot of the captain's ladder. One need not repeat at length what all of us already know about the story: that the captain's identification with Leggatt is based on a recognition of likeness—there is a lawless and impulsive Leggatt in the captain as in all law-abiding men, symbolized by the headless appearance of the swimming figure that emerges from the phosphorescent water at the foot of the rope ladder. I should like, rather, to explore two puzzling features of the story that are of especial interest. Why, indeed, does the captain have to take his ship so close to shore before coming about in order to let Leggatt slip over the side? The captain most surely knows that Leggatt must be a prodigious swimmer. And, then, what is the meaning of the final line, "my second self had lowered himself into the water to take his punishment; a free man, a proud swimmer striking out for a new destiny"?

The madly skillful maneuver of bringing the ship that close to Koh-ring has nothing to do with paying a debt to the captain's second self, but it is rather a symbolization of the crisis of competence, the third of the crises mentioned earlier. It is the captain testing his own limits, a full testing. Leggatt had already warned him of the folly of the maneuver, impulsive Leggatt: " 'Be careful,' he murmured warningly, and I realized that all my future, the only future for which I was fit, would perhaps go irretrievably to pieces in any mishap to my first command." Yet take her in he must. There is an element of Russian roulette in the scene; the same rule prevails—that to gain identity, one must risk losing it altogether. It is the rule of coping with crisis. Leggatt had set the foresail, had risked his life. He had risked his impulse of anger too, had strangled the mutinous crew member. He had lost. By putting in that close to shore the captain was in his turn playing win all or lose all. In this deepest respect they were allies. It is not surprising, then, that it is the hat, the symbol of the head and of integrity, the hat thrown to Leggatt in the water, that provides a marker by which the captain is able to judge his steerageway when he has come hard alee. The prize, when he has won, is that he is now the sole master of the ship and in a sense is rid of Leggatt, but in a very special sense.

To the captain, the departing Leggatt is a free man and a proud swimmer seeking a new destiny. It would seem that the captain had freed not only himself but the stranger as well. What has happened is that a victory of discrimination has been won. It is not that the secret sharer has been eliminated but that he has been recognized. The captain is no longer to be confused by his conflicting identities. Having risked the ordeal, he is now able to distinguish that part of himself which is the master of the ship, that part which is the double. Discriminated, the two of them are now at peace: "And I watched the hat, the expression of my sudden pity for his mere flesh. It had been meant to save his homeless head from the dangers of the sun. And now—behold—it was saving the ship. . . ." Not only is Leggatt free and proud; so too is the captain. The cast has been found, the text explicated. No despair here.

We have already commented upon the plight of Meursault, the narrator in *The Stranger*. His tragic situation, and it must be called that, is that his vision or myth of his own life—a life perceived by him as a set of self-sufficient existential moments, each providing its own meaning—does not mesh with the expectations that society lives by. The point is not that his understanding is better, or that the conventional morality and the conventional conception of cause and effect are more adequate; it is that there is no contact. And so at the critical moment of the trial, he says: "Just then I noticed that almost all the people in the courtroom were greeting each other, exchanging remarks and forming groups—behaving in fact as in a club where the company of others of one's own tastes and standing makes one feel at ease. That, no doubt, explained the odd impression I had of being *de trop* here, of being a gate crasher." And when the testimony unrolls, it seems to Meursault not to be about his life, his motives, his way of knowing the world at all. He is the stranger. And, indeed, each man is the stranger. I do not mean to be excessively clinical about the unfortunate Meursault, for it is obvious that Camus intended him as a symbol and not as a case study. Yet it is appropriate to note that there is something psychologically very special about him. Having failed to resolve what earlier we spoke of as the crisis of trust, having failed to find some meaningfulness, it is impossible for him to be concerned with any of the other crises. Initiative, competence, intimacy—all are meaningless. But in the end, like the captain, he finds his integrity in *recognizing* the indifference of the universe, washed clean of rage.

Oddly enough, I think Jules Romain's short novel, *The Death of a Nobody*, gives a clue to the special psychological quality of Camus' narrator. The novel is an extended account of what Eliot put in a metaphoric image: we die not with a bang but a whimper. A retired railroad functionary comes to a somewhat shabby section of Paris to live, contracts an illness after an expedition to the Pantheon, dies quietly in his room. The concierge and the stock characters of the neighborhood are a bit shocked, but there are few ripples. A life comes anonymously to an end. That is all that happens. I am not doing full justice to the structure of the novel, but you will recognize that it is not a very good novel, though it is a brave attempt to capture urban anonymity and man's small place in the world. Romain's hero has never committed the murder precipitating the action that permits Meursault to capture his own autonomy. He only catches cold. The main event in his life is his death: and it is absurd. Like Camus, Romain is very French. For both of them, identity includes a conception of one's place in a greater scheme, a matching of personal meaning with some external meaning. Superficially, each writer concludes that there is none, yet more deeply each asserts that whatever there is suffices. One is freer by virtue of knowing the manner in which he is a victim. Both novelists are dealing with the crisis of autonomy: one successfully, the other not, but that makes no difference here. What makes the difference is knowledge of one's predicament.

The theme repeats itself in *The Great Gatsby*, but in a different setting and with a different resolution. Gatsby seeks to be his own creator—no roots, no background, infinite facade. His parties overflow, but in the end his funeral is unattended.

And for all that, what is the true despair is that the world to which he aspires, the world he seeks to create in which to live out his dream, is not only not worth creating but that Gatsby never recognizes this: "The truth is that Jay Gatsby of West Egg, Long Island, sprang from his Platonic conception of himself. He was a son of God—a phrase which if it means anything means just that—and he must be about his Father's business, the service of a vast, vulgar, and meretricious Beauty. So he invented just the sort of Jay Gatsby that a seventeen year old boy would be likely to invent, and to this conception he was faithful to the end." And to the end he could not face or master the crises that could give him an identity beyond the Platonic facade. Daisy herself destroys the dream of Daisy. In the end, with no awareness, the web of dreams that Gatsby had tried to build into a life dissolves.

Why does the novel replace the great unifying myths? The emergence of the novel as a "character art" very likely reflects the increase in self-consciousness that has been part of the development of our civilization, as various critics have suggested. The mythic form, serving as protoscience, protoreligion, and protoliterature, depended for its full effectiveness, as we have noted, upon a sharing of beliefs about origins—supernatural origins under the control of a personalized, deified destiny such as the Greek pantheon. Drama, thaumaturgy, and science, when such a culture prevails, are not so far removed each from the other, for the form of "scientific" explanation is more often than not a dramatic or magical one.

A corollary of this proposition is that the psychological novel, in contrast to the myth, exists as a recognition of the distinction between subjective and objective. Compare the relation between Leggatt and the captain, on the one hand, and that between Agamemnon and Ajax, on the other—or contrast Meursault in *The Stranger* and Sisyphus of the myth, each coping with ultimate absurdity. The contemporary novel is subjective, immanent, living in time, animated by human impulses that lead to human actions. The myth is objective, transcendental, timeless, moved by impulses beyond man to meet inhuman demands. In the objective verisimilitude of myth lies the triumph of its externalization of man's inner experience. With the novel and its interior monologues, the effort is to save the subjectivity, to use it as cause. Meursault's sense of meaningless is not a divine condemnation: it is of his own flesh. He is not condemned, as Sisyphus was, to push the rock endlessly up a slope.

To consider the element of time in myth and the novel is revealing. Leon Edel in his *The Psychological Novel* makes much of the subjective conception of time in contemporary writing:

We know that Proust studied briefly under Bergson and that he read his works. He mentions him only once, in *Cities of the Plain*, in connection with the effects of soporific drugs on memory. Memory, however, is at the heart of Bergson's explorations, as it is of Proust's. Bergson's concept of time—*la durée*—is the measure of existence. "The invisible progress of the past, that gnaws into the future," his thesis of the use of the past in the evolution of the creative act, his discussion of intuition and reality, his belief in the flux of experience—all these ideas are taken up and studied with extraordinary refinement by Proust. Like William James, Bergson taught that we are remoulded constantly by experience; that consciousness is a process of endless accretion, so long as mind and senses are functioning; that it is "the continuation of an indefinite past in a living present." And out of this comes also the preoccupation with time which is central to the psychological novel. The watch measures off the hours with continuing regularity, but consciousness sometimes makes an hour seem like a day, or a day like an hour. In the mind past and present merge: we suddenly call up a memory of childhood that is chronologically of the distant past; but in it, memory becomes instantly vivid and is relived for the moment that it is recalled. So, in setting down in the novel the thoughts as they are passing through the mind of the character, the novelist is catching and recording the present moment—and no other. It was no accident that Joyce sought to record a single day in *Ulysses* and that throughout Virginia Woolf there is a preoccupation with "the moment." [2]

[2] *The Psychological Novel* (London: Rupert Hart-Davis, 1955), pp. 28–29.

Myth, the realm of eternal representation, on the contrary, is replete with reference to eternities. Sisyphus is eternally with his rock; Prometheus is not involved in an episode. Indeed, the decline of the Golden Age in Greek myth is in the thousands of years. Time and space are impersonal, desubjectified, as they are in the science of the nineteenth century. Science having captured time, what is left as personal is *la durée,* the length and breadth of existence as experienced.

The crises of growth with which we started, Erikson's list of human vicissitudes, are all personal, all subjective, all elementary forms of a struggle for awareness. It is the struggle for awareness that is so poignantly summarized today in our preoccupation with the "quest for identity." It is not, in turning to literature, that we seek mythic models for action. Rather, the search is for models or images or paradigms of awareness and its paradoxes: it is not objective reality and what to do when up against it, but subjective reality and how to discern it. One cannot help but compare the autobiographical fragment left by Ghiberti, discussing the long period during which he worked on the famous doors of the Baptistery at Florence, with the personal writing, say, of a modern sculptor like Henry Moore. Ghiberti talks of the material that was "needed" to do the designs that were "required." It is as if it were all "out there." Moore is concerned with the creating of illusions and symbols, and self-awareness for him is as important as a stone chisel.

The modern novel in many ways is a reflection of the separation of ways of knowing into the literary, the scientific, and the religious. While they were of a piece, the myth was an appropriate vehicle for the clarifying externalization. Today, in our age of separatism, the novel seeks an art form suitable to the changing, increasingly subjective mind of modern man.

I think the transition from myth to novel can be well illustrated by a crisis in development that comes after all of Erikson's have gone by. It is the crisis involved in facing death, in dying. There has been an attenuation of the sense and significance of death. The instructing myth has eroded. Death now is the machine stopping. Once the shades were able to pay the boatman Charon for their passage across the Styx with a coin placed under the tongue of those who had died by those who had been left behind. Today death has become somehow impersonal and unnecessary, perhaps like a fatal vitamin deficiency that might have been prevented or at least delayed. Death in the abstract has been couched in such large numbers —one hundred thousand at Hiroshima, four million Jews exterminated, the holocaust properties of the new thermo-nuclear weapons—that we have at times lost sight of what individual dying means. The wonder drugs have shed still another abstract light on dying, and one reads drug advertising with the sense that death must be an error on the part of the consumer. John Sloan Dickey, writing of the contemporary American undergraduate, remarks that, because of the scatter-ing of the extended family of great-aunts and grandparents, few have seen death close by. One dies nowadays in hospitals, hidden from view, victims of medical failure.

What has this to do with awareness of identity, with myth and novel? I would suggest in the spirit of an hypothesis that a concept of death and its dignity are always inherent in a culture that imparts a sense of meaning to life. If a life has a structure and a meaning, there must be times for dying that are more appropriate than others, ways of dying that are better than others. We must come to terms with death, and the image of the used-up machine provides no terms at all. It may well be that a sense of irreplaceability, connoting a felt uniqueness, is the hallmark of one who dies well and in continuity with life. Perhaps it is the anonymity of modern technological life that makes it so difficult, then, to have a "death of one's own." It is not as in Rilke's *Malte Laurits Brigge*, with the grandfather, Chamberlain Christoph Detlev,

roaring from room to room in the house over which he presided, dying with a desperate blend of protest and pride, yet
knowing that the coin for Charon would be under his tongue:
"It was the . . . death which the Chamberlain had carried
within time and nourished in himself his whole life long. All
excess of pride, will and lordly vigor that he himself had not
been able to consume in his quiet days had passed into his
death. . . . And when I think of the others I have seen or
about whom I have heard: it is always the same. They all have
had a death of their own."

Where technique grows without supporting compassion, as
so often happens in a transitional phase of growth in our
society, we lose sight of the cruelty of prolonging life, prolonging it because it is possible to do so and because we have been
hard put to define when, if you will, a life has been spent.
Should a man go on living though he has become a vegetable
or only a mindless vehicle of pain? "Dying should be while
there is still some taste in life to have made it worth living.
It should be while a man is still loved and before he has become a hated burden or a fool." A friend put it that way, trying
to fathom what might be meant by a "right death."

The myth of a hereafter is premised on a conception of a
persistent fate, persistent no mater how fickle its execution.
It requires a sense of the inexplicable magic of death, whether
the brooding magic or even the faery touch of E. M. Forster's
Celestial Omnibus. Technical intervention with death, however beneficent or violent, whether positively through medical
practice or negatively through man-made slaughter reckoned
in exponents, hastens the secularization of heaven into a cipher,
leaving death with the sole meaning of no-life.

There have been many learned and wise words written
about the decline in the power of the afterlife as a mythic
symbol and a guiding religious idea. To trace the history of the
decline is a monumental labor and need not concern us here.
The enlightenment and skepticism of science, the divorce of

the concept of truth from the uses of poetry and metaphor and its canonical connection with objective proof, the encroachment of a feeling of human potency on what was formerly thought of as fate—all of these have made life more valued and death more neuter. The result is an increased demand for significance in life, for a sense of identity, for meaning in experience; and with it goes a loss of tolerance for absurdity or, better, a greater readiness to recognize absurdity as an immanent property of life.

While heaven prevailed, its externalizing myth could point outward beyond experience. With its erosion, a new literary symbolism became necessary. The inventions of a Poe or a Melville, Captain Ahab with his coffin prepared, the deep undertones of death in Camus' *The Plague,* Hesse's *Death and the Lover,* Freud's death instinct, Hemingway's preoccupation with dying well—all have replaced the heavenly treatment of death and after. All have been concerned not as in classic myth with what comes after death, but with what comes before it, with the style of awareness that gives death meaning in terms of life.

Though I have illustrated my point by choosing death as an example, I might as readily have taken love or competence or guilt. In each, subjectification and the demise of fate has been the historical rule. Compare the distant screen figure of Beatrice in Dante's *Vita Nuova* with Anna Karenina, or Kafka's figures with those of the Greek myths.

The novel has turned the uses of metaphor to an exploration of the ways and models of awareness. The change is as enormous, surely, as the difference between the concept of demonic possession and the concept of neurosis—the one emphasizing an outside origin, the other emphasizing origin from within.

Art as a Mode of Knowing

 For all one's conviction that the world should be open to knowing, there are certain forms of knowledge that one fears. So it is with the subject of art and man's relationship to art as creator or beholder. It is not that one actually hopes the riddle of man will withstand the inquiry of the psychologist, nor is it the fear that knowledge will make man vulnerable to manipulation, for knowledge surely makes man proof against manipulation, too. It is neither of these things. It is more likely the fear that knowledge will negate the pleasures of innocence. This is not altogether a foolish or a sentimental attitude. For there is a deep question whether the possible meanings that emerge from an effort to explain the experience of art may not mask the real meanings of a work of art.

But risky as it is, I should like to consider four aspects of the experience of art—the connecting of experience that is the reward for grasping a work of art, the manner in which achieving understanding of a poem or picture requires an expression of human effort, what it is that is "moving" about experiencing an object of beauty, and wherein lies the generality of that which we find beautiful.

It is only fair to warn at the outset that psychology as an experimental and empirical enterprise has little to say about these matters and that Whitehead may not have been altogether wrong, though he was obscure, in suggesting that, both for the exploration of the metaphysical and the poetic, the language of the poet may be the only appropriate medium.

Connectedness. Whoever reflects recognizes that there are empty and lonely spaces between one's experiences. Perhaps these gaps are the products of reflection or at least its fruits. Indeed, the conditional tense in grammar conserves a special mode for expressing our sense of these unfilled possibilities for experience. "What would it be like if . . .?" Science, by reducing the need for empiricism with its statement of general laws, fills these gaps only partly. Given $s = gt^2/2$, we may easily know the distance traversed by any falling object in the earth's gravitational field for any length of time, however limited our direct observation of specific objects falling. What is more striking still is that the equation specifies such distance for the ideal frictionless fall, a state of nature we can never directly observe. Friction may be added to the picture in the interest of "realism," but the law of falling bodies goes beyond realism. But this is somehow not enough, and we argue with Goethe's romantic view: "Gray is all theory; green grows the golden tree of life." The general scientific law, for all its beauty, leaves the interstices as yearningly empty as before.

If you travel from Florence, where you may see in the works of Cimabue at the Uffizi the peak of the thirteenth century in Italian painting, to Padua to look at the passionate, rude forms of Giotto in the Arena Chapel, you perceive a new image and something akin to a new unity in experience. Something happens between the end of the thirteenth and the beginning of the fourteenth century, for Giotto is the new century even if he lived in the old, and that something is a gain in unity. To go from the stylized, almost iconic representations of Cimabue (Figure 1) to the powerful combination of form and impulse in Giotto (Figure 2) is to break free from well-established representation to a new, more comprehensive unity. Of course, it is in poetry that one most vividly uses the new, even bizarre juxtapositions that provide the refreshing and instructive surprises of art. If form and the expression of impulse or

1. *Cimabue, Detail of Crucifix,*
Church of San Domenico, Arezzo
(Sopr. alle Gallerie, Firenze)

2. *Giotto, Detail of Crucifixion,*
Arena Chapel, Padua
(Alinari)

feeling are suddenly fused when painting departs from its iconized conventions, it is much the same order of recombining that we know in poetry. We find in Eliot's "Prufrock," for example, not solely the vein of contempt but also a basis for compassion—for the young reader, particularly, a new unity in experience. What is this experience of unity? First one has scorn for the figure who does not dare to eat a peach, who fears the mermaids will not sing to him; and then suddenly there is also compassion for this man who fears that he has measured out his life with coffee spoons, that he should have been a pair of ragged claws.

There are perhaps two processes that yield a clue about how art achieves this connecting, this comprehensiveness. One is the construction of the tautly economical symbol, a matter to which we shall turn presently. The other is the construction and exploitation of the category of possibility, the formulated but empty category through which we search out new experience. This is a method used by both art and science. The nuclear physicist creates such empty categories out of the requirements of a theory of the nature of matter: for the nucleus of an atom to behave as it is supposed to behave, there *must* be a small particle with neither positive nor negative charge, a neutrino. The neutrino is created as a fruitful fiction. And in time a neutrino is found. But a comparable creation in art does not follow the necessities of strict logical implication. Contrast the created mythic category of centaurs, torso of man and powerful lower body of horse, with the equally untenanted class, "female presidents of the United States, past, present, and future." One is a symbolic achievement, the other a device for ticking off moderately interesting eventualities. To combine man with horse is to connect the image of man's rational gift with a renewed image of virility: sexuality and strength, the fleetness and mobility of Hermes, instinctual dignity. An image is created connecting things that were previously separate in experience, an image that bridges rationality and impulse. A centaur is not a device for exploring what it would be like if men and horses were combined in varying degree. In this respect it transcends the category of "female presidents" which is such a device and only that. The centaur is, rather, a metaphoric fusing of two spheres of experience. It is this fusing that makes Prufrock, too, a metaphoric achievement: the contemptible is also an object of compassion; two islands of experience have beneath them a single continent.

Return for a moment to the painting of Giotto. In the Christ figures of the twelfth century one sees a gradual humanizing process. The crucifixion figures at the beginning of the century are without pain, weightlessly suspended from their nails, calm-faced. Gradually, and subject to edict, Deity is permitted to suffer, stylistically, at least. But in Giotto, a new conception emerges. Here is the Christ, at the limit of endurance, coarse-haired, human, formed in suffering quite unstylized. The conception of God and of the human condition are fused. This is the Son of God, a man, not an icon. One looks at this figure: it is Man, Christ, it could be a peasant in pain. It is a set of perspectives, joined in a single class, represented. We say of this truly awesome Christ that it is a painting of great unity. But just as properly we may say that it is an experience of great unity.

Metaphor joins dissimilar experiences by finding the image or the symbol that unites them at some deeper emotional level of meaning. Its effect depends upon its capacity for getting past the literal mode of connecting, and the unsuccessful metaphor is one that either fails in finding the image or gets caught in the meshes of literalness. We may say of a woman that "she is a peach"—peach by now connoting little more than "very nice"—and the effect is prosaic. But say now of a woman that "she is a garden" and the metaphoric process is renewed, with a skein of unpredictable though not altogether pleasing affective connections.

For, indeed, there is more to the metaphor of art than mere emotional connectedness. There is also the canon of economy that must operate, a canon that distinguishes the artfully metaphoric from that which is only floridly arty or simply "offbeat." It is the difference between the chaste interior of the Salzburg Dreifalltigskeitkirche of the young Fischer von Erlach, with the graceful oval of its cupola surmounted by a dove, and the heavily florid profusion of marbles of his later Karlskirche in Vienna. The first speaks quietly through its sparsely decorated geometry of man's celebration of a sophisticated Deity; the other merely boasts in opulence. Or it is the difference between an elaborate ceremonial canvas depicting the blend of power and piety of the sixteenth-century church and a painting by El Greco of one of its cruel and pious cardinals (Figure 3).

Though the idea of economy in metaphor is by no means novel, it is worth special mention in a discussion of art as knowing, for it is precisely in its economy that art shares a

3. El Greco, *Portrait of Cardinal Guevara*, Metropolitan Museum,
New York. Bequest of Mrs. H. O. Havemeyer, 1929. The
H. O. Havemeyer Collection.

fundamental principle with other forms of knowing. There is, perhaps, one universal truth about all forms of human cognition: the ability to deal with knowledge is hugely exceeded by the potential knowledge contained in man's environment. To cope with this diversity, man's perception, his memory, and his thought processes early become governed by strategies for protecting his limited capacities from the confusion of overloading. We tend to perceive things schematically, for example, rather than in detail, or we represent a class of diverse things by some sort of averaged "typical instance." The corresponding principle of economy in art produces the compact image or symbol that, by its genius, travels great distances to connect ostensible disparities.

Lest it seem that the modes of connecting in art and science are separated by an unbridgeable gap, that in all ways they are different modes of knowing, one primitive similarity should be mentioned—one that partakes of the nature of metaphor. It is the manner in which the scientist gets his hypothesis. Philosophers of science, who, characteristically, do not practice science but only reflect upon its more public forms of discipline, rarely touch on this theme. For these worthy men the labors of the scientist often begin with an hypothesis to be verified, or at least with rules of induction for discriminating nature's signal from her noise. Or, at even a further remove, they are concerned with the subtle and beautiful process of formalizing knowledge into the special symbolic language of mathematics. Yet the prescientific effort to construct a fruitful hypothesis may indeed be the place where the art of science, like all other art forms, operates by the law of economical metaphor. May it not be that without the myth of Sisyphus, forever pushing his rock up the hill, the concept of the asymptote in mathematics would be less readily grasped? What is Heraclitus' account but a giant metaphor on instability? He gropes for a picture of the universe. And so it is at the beginnings of insight. In a later chapter, we shall consider Freud

and the dramatic metaphor that made his first steps possible.
So too in the other newer sciences that are in search of guiding
"pictures." Surely the "mental evolution" conceived by the
early anthropologists could only be taken in a metaphoric
sense, for there is patently no correspondence between evolutionary genetics and the manner in which so biologically stable
a race as man should emerge culturally from the savage state
to the writing of philosophy. As Bertrand Russell comments,
"Physics is mathematical not because we know so much about
the physical world, but because we know so little: it is only its
mathematical properties that we can discover." And until they
are "discovered" in this more rigorous sense, one proceeds by
intuition and metaphor, hoping to be led beyond to a new
rigor. Until then, the economical combinings of the scientist
and the artist share far more than we are often prepared to
admit.

Effort. The art historian Ernst Gombrich, lecturing before
an august group of British psychoanalysts, used an interesting illustration to underscore the role of work in aesthetic
pleasure. He presented a very ordinary academic painting by
Bonnencontre, typical of French academic technique of the
final quarter of the last century (Figure 4). It is not a very
pleasing piece of work and certainly not a moving one. Gom-

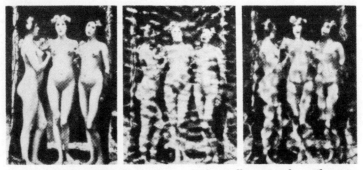

4. Bonnencontre, *The Three Graces, Soho Gallery, London. The two
reproductions on the right are seen as through rolled glass.* "Psychoanalysis and the History of Art," Int. J. Psych., 1954. (*Braun et Cie*)

brich then presented the picture covered with unevenly rolled, transparent glass, which had the effect of breaking up the idealized forms and the planes of the surface in much the same way as John Marin learned to do in his water colors. The effect was most striking. The picture was now interesting, and with an effort something could be made of it.

What is this effort? Perhaps it consists in departing from the habitual and literal ways of looking, hearing, and understanding in order to resolve the ambiguity that is a feature of works of art. But in a deeper sense, it is the effort to make a new connection between different perspectives. The trick used by Gombrich prevents an easy and literal perception of Bonnencontre's figures and forces the metaphoric mode on the beholder. This happens also when one encounters both piety and cruelty in an El Greco cardinal. What one feels is the effort to connect. It is not only for the creation of a work of art that one should use the expression *unitas multiplex,* but for the experience of knowing it as well.

But why is one willing to undertake the effort? Perhaps the effort of beholding art is its own reward, or the reward is the achievement of unity of experience, which is to say that it develops on itself. Taste begets better taste. Listen to enough Dvorak and a taste for Beethoven or Wagner will develop. If ever there were a pure instance of what Karl Bühler long ago called *Funktionslust,* pleasure in the exercise of a function, the realm of art is its home.

Somehow the image of the beholder of a painting as one who works, however much he enjoys his work and is rewarded by the enrichment it affords, is too Puritan an image. There is much in art that is undemandingly decorative. Does this differ from the kind of art we have been considering? Shall we honor the distinction Graham Greene makes between his "novels" and his "entertainments"? I think so. And I believe that the distinction is precisely in terms of the amount and the nature of the work demanded.

I happen to have a favorite period of decorative painting, that of the great Sienese school, and my particular favorite is Sassetta. Perhaps I shall sound insufficiently appreciative of such painting, but I am not. It has an elegant restfulness. Faith, Hope, and Charity ascending into the heavens in defiance of the laws of gravity are incomparably and uncomplicatedly feminine (Figure 5), and one loves this painting of St. Francis taking his vows to Poverty in the way that one loves to go back to innocent ways of hearing the fairy stories of childhood. For Sassetta's canvas to create the disturbance of art, to go from being decorative to being powerfully beautiful, there must be an infusion of productive paradox. For it is this that triggers the work of connecting. This is not to say that the work is enough. It must surely result, if successful, in the self-rewarding experience of connection.

But creating new unities is not all the work. There is also control and conversion of the impulses that are aroused in the experience of art, the exercise of restraint that permits the reader to maintain a distance from the hero of a novel and the playgoer to remain on his side of the proscenium arch. Here again the distinction between the decorative and beautiful is useful. For the decorative achieves its restfulness by permitting us to remain uninvolved, untempted. Indeed, an essay remains to be written on the defense against beauty, about those who, in the face of the awesomeness of a Gothic cathedral, can remain unshaken and find what they behold merely pleasing. But these are matters better treated more systematically, and to this we turn now.

Conversion of impulse. Any impulse, we have argued, can be turned to art: the urge to kill becomes the art of rudeness; curiosity produces the art of conversation; sexuality matures into the art of making love. It is a necessary but not a sufficient condition in each case that the impulse be held in check and converted from its original form. It is equally true that the successful *beholding* of a work of art involves a comparable

5. Sassetta, *Marriage of St. Francis and Poverty, Musée Conde, Chantilly*
(*Bulloz*)

act of containing impulses that have been aroused. It is not necessary that there be a concordance in the impulse of the creator and the beholder, and, for our purposes, the matter of communicating an impulse from creator to receiver is not at issue.

Consider the beautiful piece of Renaissance statuary in the Toledo Cathedral known as the Santa Maria Blanca, a graceful half-smiling Virgin holding the Christ Child, who reaches up as if to chuck her under the chin (Figure 6). This White Virgin is all the faces of woman, mother, wife, flirt, daughter, sister, mistress, saint, and harlot. As one looks at it, there are impulses-in-restraint to father her, be mothered by her, make love to her, gossip with her, and just to watch how the face will change when the Child finally pokes her under the chin. It provides a fine example, for probably the conversion of impulse into a sense of beauty requires the arousing of several impulses at once. And here, if anywhere, one may speak of the experience of art as a mode of knowing. For when one looks at the White Virgin, the energy of all one's discordant impulses creates a single image connecting the varieties of experience in her extraordinary face.

Let us be more specific about how impulses are converted into the experience of art. Two types of cognitive activity are set in train when a need is aroused. One is at the center of awareness as desire: it is directed toward achieving an end and is specialized to the task of finding means. The other is at the fringes of awareness, a flow of rich and surprising fantasy, a tangled reticle of associations that gives fleeting glimpses of past occasions, of disappointments and triumphs, of pleasure and unpleasures. It is the stuff of which James's stream of consciousness was made, and we honor such a writer as Joyce for his insight into the technical problem of communicating this scarcely expressible fringe. To the degree that the direct expression of impulse can be kept in abeyance, to that degree it is possible for the fringes of association to elaborate themselves. And to this degree too there can be a merging of the

6. *Santa Maria Blanca, The Cathedral, Toledo. Three views.*

streams fed by different impulses, a joining of the scraps and images. For at this level, thinking is more symphonic than logical, one theme suggesting the next by a rule of letting parts stand for wholes. Where art achieves its genius is in providing an image or a symbol whereby the fusion can be comprehended and bound.

In short, the conversion of impulse into the experience of art comes from the creation of a stream of metaphoric activity and the restraining of any direct striving for ends. In essence, the connecting of experience is given its first impetus by the simultaneous presence of several such streams of fringe association. It is the formal artifice of the work of art itself, the genius of its economical imagery, that makes possible the final fusing of these inner experiences. The process we have described requires work from the beholder. Beholding an art object in a manner that may be called knowing is not a passive act. But when the beholder stops beholding, when there is too much involvement with the figures in a canvas, there is an end to the conversion of impulse, distance is lost, and in place of the experience of art there is either a daydream or merely action.

Generality. Any idea, any construct or metaphor, has its range of convenience or its "fit" to experience, and this is one feature that art and science as modes of knowing share deeply. A concept like "parthenogenesis," for example, fits certain reproductive phenomena in biology, but fails to fit or predict others. Our techniques for finding out about the range of convenience of ideas in science are rather straightforward, though it requires much ingenuity at times to devise operational techniques for verification. There is no direct analogue of verification in the experience of art. In its place, there is a "shock of recognition," a recognition of the fittingness of an object or a poem to fill the gaps in our own experience. In this sense, and it is a limited sense, we may say that art is not a universal mode of communication, for each man who beholds a picture or reads a poem will bring to the experience a matrix of life that is uniquely his own. Though this is certainly the case, and though it is true that one's vision of the Santa Maria Blanca may not be the same as that of the sexton who lights the evening candles in the Toledo Cathedral, it is equally true to say that there are constant features of the human situation and that for all men there is the problem of reconciling the different faces of woman: harlot with wife, flirt with mother, and the rest. For one beholder this exquisite piece of Renaissance statuary may engage with this need for reconciliation, for another not. The predicament is differently shaped for each: for the intransigently religious man the Virgin and Child may pre-empt the entire experience.

This is scarcely to say that the communicability of a work of art is a function entirely of time, place, and condition. For if it were, one would not find such a shock of refreshment in the cave paintings of Altamira and Lascaux or in the artifacts of the second Pueblo period. One need not invoke a racial unconscious or archetypal images to account for this communicability across cultures and times: there are features of the human condition that change only within narrow limits whether one be a cave dweller, a don in medieval Oxford, or a Left Bank expatriate of the 1920s: love, birth, hate, death, passion, and decorum persist as problems without unique solution.

Can it ever be said, then, that life imitates art? If so, then art is the furthest reach of communication. There are perhaps two ways that are somewhat more than trivial. One is the effect of art in freeing us from the forms of instrumental knowing that comprise the center of our awareness; from the tendency to say that this figure here represents Christ, that over there is an apple; apples are good for eating, Christ for worshiping or admiring. When we see the possibility of connection in internal experience, we strive to recreate it and to live it.

The second sense in which life imitates art is in the manner in which the experience of art nourishes itself, so that having sensed connectedness one is impelled to seek more of it.

James Bryant Conant, presiding some years ago over a meeting of the Harvard faculty which was debating the relationship between engineering sciences and applied physics, remarked that the object of a science is to reduce empiricism. The intent of the scientist is to create rational structures and general laws that, in the mathematical sense, predict the observations one would be forced to make if one were without the general laws. To the degree that the rational structures of science are governed by principles of strict logical implication, to that degree prediction becomes more and more complete, leading eventually to the derivation of possible observations that one might not have made but for the existence of the general theory. Surely, then, science increases the unity of our experience of nature. This is the hallmark of the way of knowing called science.

Art as a form of knowing does not and cannot strive for such a form of unification. In its most refined form, the myth of Sisyphus is not the concept of the mathematical asymptote. The elegant rationality of science and the metaphoric non-rationality of art operate with deeply different grammars; perhaps they even represent a profound complementarity. For in the experience of art, we connect by a grammar of metaphor, one that defies the rational methods of the linguist and the psychologist. There has been progress in interpreting the metaphoric transformation of dreams, rendering the latent meaning from the manifest content, progress to which Freud contributed so greatly. Yet to interpret a dream as "a wish to be loved by one's rejecting mother" or to interpret Marlow's pursuit of Kurtz at the end of Conrad's "Heart of Darkness" as a man pursuing a bride, neither of these exercises, however revealing, catches fully the nature of metaphor. What is lost in such translations is the very fullness of the connection produced by the experience of art itself.

PART II

the Quest for Clarity

The essays that follow—"The Act of Discovery," "On Learning Mathematics," and "After John Dewey, What?"—are all ostensibly concerned with the process of education. But education is a process that cannot, I think, be separated from what it is that one seeks to teach. It is much as in the study of the nature of knowing: one cannot pursue the investigation of how one comes to know without full heed of what it is that is known. It has always been disturbing to me that some psychologists have operated on the assumption that knowing anything is the same as knowing anything else—a pigeon pecking buttons discriminatively or a rat finding his way through a maze or an undergraduate withdrawing his finger from a switch when a light appeared represent the componentry out of which any higher order of knowledge is constructed. Perhaps I can sum up my dissent by the overly simple dictum that the whole is less than the sum of the parts. A house is not a matter of knowing about a collection of nails, shingles, wallboards, and windows. Nor can it be said that it is *more* than these things, for to say this is to make it seem that the organization of elements produces something more complex than the sum of these elements. Instead, higher-order mental organization, or cognitive structure as it is sometimes called, has the effect of supplanting the niggling complexities and Irish pennants of the less good orders that precede the imposition of more encompassing orders on experience.

If, then, the structure of knowledge has its own laws, makes its own contribution to the economical use of mind, one must necessarily look to such a structure for hints about the nature and uses of mind. If it is the case that the power and significance of poetry resides in its capacity to condense and symbolize experience in a well-wrought metaphoric web, then it follows that the teaching of poetry must honor the nature of poetry by providing the learner an opportunity to discover and use its special powers. And so too with mathematics or any "subject" one chooses to understand or to teach.

So, though the essays that follow are ostensibly about teaching and learning, they are also about the nature of knowing and about the nature of things to be known. They are perhaps more "right-handed" than the essays that precede them, largely because they are more closely related to some of my most horny-handed experimental studies of perception, memory, and thinking—notably the work reported in *A Study of Thinking* (New York: John Wiley, 1956) and in *Contemporary Approaches to Cognition* (Cambridge: Harvard University Press, 1957).

"The Act of Discovery" first took form after my having seen two inspired teachers of mathematics at work at the University School of the University of Illinois—David Page and Max Beberman. Both of them practiced the canny art of intellectual temptation, and in a few hours I saw quite ordinary students in their classes discovering quite unself-consciously all manner of interesting mathematical relations. There is an informal seminar at Illinois made up of educators, psychologists, mathematicians, chemists, physicists, and others who care actively about how one teaches anything. My friend Lee Cronbach asked me if I would talk with the group about what had struck me in my visit. The seminar went on for many hours, and the basis of the essay published here is the set of notes I took then. It was later presented in a somewhat different form in an address to the Society for the Philosophy of Education and published in yet a different form in the *Harvard Educational Review* (Winter 1961).

"On Learning Mathematics" is, among other things, a summer conversation with my step-daughter Lyn who, during its preparation, was getting ready to go off to Uganda to teach mathematics at the Demonstration School in Kampala. It was a summer in which there was much talk at home about how one gets children to think mathematically. I had been invited to talk before the National Council of Teachers of Mathematics; the conversations at home, correspondence with David Page, and the invitation all conspired to get me much involved in thinking about the tactics and strategy of mathematics teaching as a special and interesting case of teaching and learning. The following year I was also committed to a joint research project with the English mathematician, Z. P. Dienes, designed to investigate the nature of conceptual learning in mathematics. "On Learning Mathematics" served to clear my mind on some of the issues we were to face. Today I could not write the essay in its present form. "Mathematics learning" is now a right-handed subject for me, but the essay included here was a left-handed propaedeutic to what followed. The essay, in slightly altered form, first appeared in *The Mathematics Teacher* (December 1960).

The John Dewey piece appeared first in the *Saturday Review* (Suppl., June 17, 1961), and its origin is amusing. My wife and I had gone to Toronto in mid-winter to take part in a conference on revising the curriculum of the city schools. It was a joint enterprise of the university there and the board of education, and I had been asked to come because the Toronto project had been influenced by the work of the Woods Hole Conference reported in my *The Process of Education*. It took us three days of waiting in airports and circling helplessly in weather-bound airplanes to get back to Cambridge. Through good fortune, I happened to have with me John Dewey's *My Pedagogic Creed*. I read it aloud to my wife, with comments of course. I think she must have had a certain amount of difficulty figuring out which were my comments and which was text, for in the end she suggested that I write out my thoughts on the subject as an exercise in finding out what my own credo was. I did. She was quite right.

The Act of Discovery

 Maimonides, in his *Guide for the Perplexed*, speaks of four forms of perfection that men might seek.[1] The first and lowest form is perfection in the acquisition of worldly goods. The great philosopher dismisses this on the ground that the possessions one acquires bear no meaningful relation to the possessor: "A great king may one morning find that there is no difference between him and the lowest person." A second perfection is of the body, its conformation and skills. Its failing is that it does not reflect on what is uniquely human about man: "he could (in any case) not be as strong as a mule." Moral perfection is the third, "the highest degree of excellency in man's character." Of this perfection Maimonides says: "Imagine a person being alone, and having no connection whatever with any other person; all his good moral principles are at rest, they are not required and give man no perfection whatever. These principles are only necessary and useful when man comes in contact with others." The fourth kind of perfection is "the true perfection of man; the possession of the highest intellectual faculties. . . ." In justification of his assertion, this extraordinary Spanish-Judaic philosopher urges: "Examine the first three kinds of perfection; you will find that if you possess them, they are not your property, but the property of others. . . . But the last kind of perfection is exclusively yours; no one else owns any part of it."

[1] Maimonides, *Guide for the Perplexed* (New York: Dover Publications, 1956).

Without raising the question of whether moral qualities exist without reference to others, it is a conjecture much like the last of Maimonides' that leads me to examine the act of discovery in man's intellectual life. For if man's intellectual excellence is the most his own among his perfections, it is also the case that the most personal of all that he knows is that which he has discovered for himself. How important is it, then, for us to encourage the young to learn by discovery? Does it, as Maimonides would say, create a unique relation between knowledge and its possessor? And what may such a relation do for a man—or, for our purposes, a child?

The immediate occasion for my concern with discovery is the work of the various new curriculum projects that have grown up in America during the last few years. Whether one speaks to mathematicians or physicists or historians, one encounters repeatedly an expression of faith in the powerful effects that come from permitting the student to put things together for himself, to be his own discoverer.

First, I should be clear about what the act of discovery entails. It is rarely, on the frontier of knowledge or elsewhere, that new facts are "discovered" in the sense of being encountered, as Newton suggested, in the form of islands of truth in an uncharted sea of ignorance. Or if they appear to be discovered in this way, it is almost always thanks to some happy hypothesis about where to navigate. Discovery, like surprise, favors the well-prepared mind. In playing bridge, one is surprised by a hand with no honors in it and also by one that is all in one suit. Yet all particular hands in bridge are equiprobable: to be surprised one must know something about the laws of probability. So too in discovery. The history of science is studded with examples of men "finding out" something and not knowing it. I shall operate on the assumption that discovery, whether by a schoolboy going it on his own or by a scientist cultivating the growing edge of his field, is in its essence a matter of rearranging or transforming evidence in such a way that one is enabled to go beyond the evidence so reassembled to new insights. It may well be that an additional fact or shred of evidence makes this larger transformation possible. But it is often not even dependent on new information.

Very generally, and at the risk of oversimplification, it is useful to distinguish two kinds of teaching: that which takes place in the *expository mode* and that in the *hypothetical mode*. In the former, the decisions concerning the mode and pace and style of exposition are principally determined by the teacher as expositor; the student is the listener. The speaker has a quite different set of decisions to make: he has a wide choice of alternatives; he is anticipating paragraph content while the listener is still intent on the words; he is manipulating the content of the material by various transformations while the listener is quite unaware of these internal options. But in the hypothetical mode the teacher and the student are in a more cooperative position with respect to what in linguistics would be called "speaker's decisions." The student is not a bench-bound listener, but is taking a part in the formulation and at times may play the principal role in it. He will be aware of alternatives and may even have an "as if" attitude toward these, and he may evaluate information as it comes. One cannot describe the process in either mode with great precision of detail, but I think it is largely the hypothetical mode which characterizes the teaching that encourages discovery.

Consider now what benefits might be derived from the experience of learning through discoveries that one makes oneself. I shall discuss these under four headings: (1) the increase in intellectual potency, (2) the shift from extrinsic to intrinsic rewards, (3) the learning of the heuristics of discovering, and (4) the aid to conserving memory.

Intellectual potency. I should like to consider the differences among students in a highly constrained psychological experiment involving a two-choice machine.[2] In order to win chips, they must depress a key either on the right or the left

[2] J. S. Bruner, J. J. Goodnow, and G. A. Austin, *A Study of Thinking* (New York: John Wiley, 1956).

side of the apparatus. A pattern of payoff is designed so that, say, they will be paid off on the right side 70 percent of the time, on the left 30 percent, but this detail is not important. What is important is that the payoff sequence is arranged at random, that there is no pattern. There is a marked contrast in the behavior of subjects who think that there is some pattern to be found in the sequence—who think that regularities are discoverable—and the performance of subjects who think that things are happening quite by chance. The first group adopts what is called an "event-matching" strategy in which the number of responses given to each side is roughly commensurate to the proportion of times that it pays off: in the present case, 70 on the right to 30 on the left. The group that believes there is no pattern very soon settles for a much more primitive strategy allocating *all* responses to the side that has the greater payoff. A little arithmetic will show that the lazy all-and-none strategy pays off more if the environment is truly random: they win 70 percent of the time. The event-matching subjects win about 70 percent on the 70-percent payoff side (or 49 percent of the time there) and 30 percent of the time on the side that pays off 30 percent of the time (another 9 percent for a total take-home wage of 58 percent in return for their labors of decision).

But the world is not always or not even frequently random, and if one analyzes carefully what the event matchers are doing, one sees that they are trying out hypotheses one after the other, all of them containing a term that leads to a distribution of bets on the two sides with a frequency to match the actual occurrence of events. If it should turn out that there is a pattern to be discovered, their payoff could become 100 percent. The other group would go on at the middling rate of 70 percent.

What has this to do with the subject at hand? For the person to search out and find regularities and relationships in his environment, he must either come armed with an expectancy that there will be something to find or be aroused to such an expectancy so that he may devise ways of searching and finding. One of the chief enemies of search is the assumption that there is nothing one can find in the environment by way of regularity or relationship. In the experiment just cited, subjects often fall into one of two habitual attitudes: either that there is nothing to be found or that a pattern can be discovered by looking. There is an important sequel in behavior to the two attitudes.

We have conducted a series of experimental studies on a group of some seventy schoolchildren over a four-year period.[3] The studies have led us to distinguish an interesting dimension of cognitive activity that can be described as ranging from *episodic empiricism* at one end to *cumulative constructionism* at the other. The two attitudes in the above experiments on choice illustrate the extremes of the dimension. One of the experiments employs the game of Twenty Questions. A child—in this case he is between ten and twelve—is told that a car has gone off the road and hit a tree. He is to ask questions that can be answered by "yes" or "no" to discover the cause of the accident. After completing the problem, the same task is given him, though this time he is told that the accident has a different cause. In all, the procedure is repeated four times. Children enjoy playing the game. They also differ quite markedly in the approach or strategy they bring to the task. In the first place, we can distinguish clearly between two types of questions asked: one is intended to locate constraints in the problem, constraints that will eventually give shape to an hypothesis; the other is the hypothesis as question. It is the difference between, "Was there anything wrong with the driver?" and "Was the driver rushing to the doctor's office for an appointment and the car got out of control?" There are children who precede hypotheses with efforts to locate constraint and there

[3] J. S. Bruner and others, *The Processes of Cognitive Development*, in preparation.

are those who are "potshotters," who string out hypotheses noncumulatively one after the other. A second element of strategy lies in the connectivity of information gathering: the extent to which questions asked utilize or ignore or violate information previously obtained. The questions asked by children tend to be organized in cycles, each cycle usually given over to the pursuit of some particular notion. Both within cycles and between cycles one can discern marked differences in the connectivity of the children's performances. Needless to say, children who employ constraint location as a technique preliminary to the formulation of hypotheses tend to be far more organized in their harvesting of information. Persistence is another feature of strategy, a characteristic compounded of what appear to be two factors: sheer doggedness and a persistence that stems from the sequential organization that a child brings to the task. Doggedness is probably just animal spirits or the need to achieve. Organized persistence is a maneuver for protecting the fragile cognitive apparatus from overload. The child who has flooded himself with disorganized information from unconnected hypotheses will become discouraged and confused sooner than the child who has shown a certain cunning in his strategy of getting information—a child who senses that the value of information is not simply in getting it but in being able to carry it. The persistence of the organized child stems from his knowledge of how to organize questions in cycles and how to summarize things to himself.

Episodic empiricism is illustrated by information gathering that is unbound by prior constraints, that is deficient in organizational persistence. The opposite extreme, what we have called cumulative constructionism, is characterized by sensitivity to constraint, by connective maneuvers, and by organized persistence. Brute persistence seems to be one of those gifts from the gods that make people more exaggeratedly what they are.

Before returning to the issue of discovery and its role in the development of thinking, there is a word more to say about the ways in which the problem solver may transform information he has dealt with actively. The point arises from the pragmatic question: what does it take to get information processed into a form best designed to fit some future use? An experiment by R. B. Zajonc in 1957 suggests an answer.[4] He gave groups of students information of a controlled kind, some groups being told that they were to transmit the information later on, others that they were merely to keep it in mind. In general, he found more differentiation of the information intended for transmittal than of information received passively. An active attitude leads to a transformation related to a task to be performed. There is a risk, to be sure, in the possible overspecialization of information processing. It can lead to such a high degree of specific organization that information is lost for general use, although this can be guarded against.

Let me convert the foregoing into an hypothesis. Emphasis on discovery in learning has precisely the effect on the learner of leading him to be a constructionist, to organize what he is encountering in a manner not only designed to discover regularity and relatedness, but also to avoid the kind of information drift that fails to keep account of the uses to which information might have to be put. Emphasis on discovery, indeed, helps the child to learn the varieties of problem solving, of transforming information for better use, helps him to learn how to go about the very task of learning. So goes the hypothesis; it is still in need of testing. But it is an hypothesis of such important human implications that we cannot afford not to test it—and the testing will have to be in the schools.

Intrinsic and extrinsic motives. Much of the problem in leading a child to effective cognitive activity is to free him from the immediate control of environmental rewards and punishments. Learning that starts in response to the rewards of parental or teacher approval or to the avoidance of failure can

[4] R. B. Zajonc, personal communication (1957).

too readily develop a pattern in which the child is seeking cues as to how to conform to what is expected of him. We know from studies of children who tend to be early overachievers in school that they are likely to be seekers after the "right way to do it" and that their capacity for transforming learning into viable thought structures tends to be lower than that of children achieving at levels predicted by intelligence tests.[5] Our tests on such children show them to be lower in analytic ability than those who are not conspicuous in overachievement. As we shall see later, they develop rote abilities and depend on being able to "give back" what is expected rather than to make it into something that relates to the rest of their cognitive life. As Maimonides would say, their learning is not their own.

The hypothesis I would propose here is that to the degree that one is able to approach learning as a task of discovering something rather than "learning about" it, to that degree there will be a tendency for the child to work with the autonomy of self-reward or, more properly, be rewarded by discovery itself.

To readers familiar with the battles of the last half-century in the field of motivation, this hypothesis will be recognized as controversial. For the traditional view of motivation in learning has been, until very recently, couched in terms of a theory of drives and reinforcements: learning occurs because a response produced by a stimulus is followed by the reduction in a primary drive. The doctrine is greatly but thinly extended by the idea of secondary reinforcement: anything that has been "associated" with such a reduction in drive or need can also serve to reinforce the connection between a stimulus and the response that it evokes. Finding a steak will do for getting a food-search act connected with a certain stimulus, but so will the sight of a nice restaurant.

In 1959 there appeared a most searching and important criticism of this ancient hedonistic position, written by Robert White, reviewing the evidence of recently published animal studies, of work in the field of psychoanalysis, and of research

[5] See Note 3 above.

on the development of cognitive processes in children. Professor White comes to the conclusion, quite rightly I think, that the drive-reduction model of learning runs counter to too many important phenomena of learning and development to be either regarded as general in its applicability or even correct in its general approach. Let me quote some of his principal conclusions and explore their applicability to the hypothesis stated above.

I now propose that we gather the various kinds of behavior just mentioned, all of which have to do with effective interaction with the environment, under the general heading of competence. According to Webster, competence means fitness of ability, and the suggested synonyms include capability, capacity, efficiency, proficiency, and skill. It is therefore a suitable word to describe such things as grasping and exploring, crawling and walking, attention and perception, language and thinking, manipulating and changing the surroundings, all of which promote an effective—a competent—interaction with the environment. It is true, of course, that maturation plays a part in all these developments, but this part is heavily overshadowed by learning in all the more complex accomplishments like speech or skilled manipulation. I shall argue that it is necessary to make competence a motivational concept; there is *competence motivation* as well as competence in its more familiar sense of achieved capacity. The behavior that leads to the building up of effective grasping, handling, and letting go of objects, to take one example, is not random behavior that is produced by an overflow of energy. It is directed, selective, and persistent, and it continues not because it serves primary drives, which indeed it cannot serve until it is almost perfected, but because it satisfies an intrinsic need to deal with the environment.[6]

I am suggesting that there are forms of activity that serve to enlist and develop the competence motive, that serve to make it the driving force behind behavior. I should like to add to White's general premise that the *exercise* of competence motives has the effect of strengthening the degree to which they gain control over behavior and thereby reduce the effects of extrinsic rewards or drive gratification.

In 1934 the brilliant Russian psychologist Vygotsky charac-

[6] R. W. White, "Motivation Reconsidered: The Concept of Competence," *Psychological Review*, no. 66 (1959), pp. 317–318.

terized the growth of thought processes as starting with a dialogue of speech and gesture between child and parent.[7] Autonomous thinking, he said, begins at the stage when the child is first able to internalize these conversations and "run them off" himself. This is a typical sequence in the development of competence. So too in instruction. The narrative of teaching is of the order of Vygotsky's conversation. The next move in the development of competence is the internalization of the narrative and its "rules of generation" so that the child is now capable of running off the narrative on his own. The hypothetical mode in teaching, by encouraging the child to participate in "speaker's decisions," speeds this process along. Once internalization has occurred, the child is in a vastly improved position from several obvious points of view—notably that he is able to go beyond the information he has been given to generate additional ideas that either can be checked immediately from experience or can, at least, be used as a basis for formulating reasonable hypotheses. But over and beyond that, the child is now in a position to experience success and failure not as reward and punishment but as information. For when the task is his own rather than a prescribed matching of environmental demands, he becomes his own paymaster in a certain measure. Seeking to gain control over his environment, he can now treat success as indicating that he is on the right track, failure as indicating that he is on the wrong one.

In the end, this development has the effect of freeing learning from immediate stimulus control. When learning leads only to pellets of this or that in the short run rather than to mastery in the long run, then behavior can be readily "shaped" by extrinsic rewards. But when behavior becomes more extended and competence-oriented, it comes under the control of more complex cognitive structures and operates more from the inside out.

The position of Pavlov is interesting. His early account of

[7] L. S. Vygotsky, *Thinking and Speech* (Moscow, 1934).

the learning process was based entirely on a notion of stimulus control of behavior through the conditioning mechanism in which, through contiguity, a new conditioned stimulus was substituted for an old unconditioned stimulus. But even he recognized that his account was insufficient to deal with higher forms of learning. To supplement it, he introduced the idea of the "second signalling system," with central importance placed on symbolic systems, such as language, in mediating and giving shape to mental life. Or as Luria put it in 1959, the first signal system is "concerned with directly perceived stimuli, the second with systems of verbal elaboration." Luria, commenting on the importance of the transition from first to second signal system, says:

It would be mistaken to suppose that verbal intercourse with adults merely changes the contents of the child's conscious activity without changing its form. . . . The word has a basic function not only because it indicates a corresponding object in the external world, but also because it abstracts, isolates the necessary signal, generalizes perceived signals and relates them to certain categories; it is this systematization of direct experience that makes the role of the word in the formation of mental processes so exceptionally important.[8]

It is interesting too that the final rejection of the universality of the doctrine of reinforcement in direct conditioning came from some of Pavlov's own students. Ivanov-Smolensky and Krasnogorsky published papers showing the manner in which symbolized linguistic messages could take over the place of the unconditioned stimulus and of the unconditioned response (gratification of hunger) in children.[9] In all instances, they

[8] A. L. Luria, "The Directive Function of Speech in Development and Dissolution," *Word*, no. 15 (1959), p. 12.

[9] A. G. Ivanov-Smolensky, "The Interaction of the First and Second Signal Systems in Certain Normal and Pathological Conditions," *Physiological Journal of the USSR*, XXXV, no. 5 (1949); Ivanov-Smolensky, "Concerning the Study of the Joint Activity of the First and Second Signal Systems," *Journal of Higher Nervous Activity*, I, no. 1 (1951); N. I. Krasnogorsky, *Studies of Higher Nervous Activity in Animals and in Man*, I (Moscow, 1954).

speak of these as *replacements* of lower first-system mental or neural processes by higher second-system controls. A strange irony, then, that Russian psychology, which gave us the notion of the conditioned response and the assumption that higher-order activities are built up out of colligations of such primitive units, has rejected this notion while much of the American psychology of learning until quite recently has stayed within the early Pavlovian fold—as, for example, a 1959 article by Spence in the *Harvard Educational Review*, reiterating the primacy of conditioning and the derivative nature of complex learning.[10] It is even more noteworthy that Russian pedagogic theory has become deeply influenced by this new trend and is now placing much stress upon the importance of building up a more active symbolical approach to problem solving among children.

In this matter of the control of learning, then, my conclusion is that the degree to which the desire for competence comes to control behavior, to that degree the role of reinforcement or "outside rewards" wanes in shaping behavior. The child comes to manipulate his environment more actively and achieves his gratification from coping with problems. As he finds symbolic modes of representing and transforming the environment, there is an accompanying decline in the importance of stimulus-response-reward sequences. To use the metaphor that David Riesman developed in a quite different context, mental life moves from a state of outer-directedness, in which the fortuity of stimuli and reinforcement are crucial, to a state of inner-directedness in which the growth and maintenance of mastery become central and dominant.

The heuristics of discovery. Lincoln Steffens, reflecting in his *Autobiography* on his undergraduate education at Berkeley, comments that his schooling paid too much attention to learning what was known and too little to finding out about what

[10] K. W. Spence, "The Relation of Learning Theory to the Technique of Education," *Harvard Educational Review,* no. 29 (1959), pp. 84–95.

was not known.[11] But how does one train a student in the techniques of discovery? Again there are some hypotheses to offer. There are many ways of coming to the arts of inquiry. One of them is by careful study of its formalization in logic, statistics, mathematics, and the like. If one is going to pursue inquiry as a way of life, particularly in the sciences, certainly such study is essential. Yet whoever has taught kindergarten and the early primary grades or has had graduate students working with him on their theses—I choose the two extremes for they are both periods of intense inquiry—knows that an understanding of the formal aspect of inquiry is not sufficient. Rather, several activities and attitudes, some directly related to a particular subject and some fairly generalized, appear to go with inquiry and research. These have to do with the *process* of trying to find out something and, though their presence is no guarantee that the *product* will be a great discovery, their absence is likely to lead to awkwardness or aridity or confusion. How difficult it is to describe these matters—the heuristics of inquiry. There is one set of attitudes or methods that has to do with sensing the relevance of variables—avoiding immersion in edge effects and getting instead to the big sources of variance. This gift partly comes from intuitive familiarity with a range of phenomena, sheer "knowing the stuff." But it also comes out of a sense of what things among many "smell right," what things are of the right order of magnitude or scope or severity.

Weldon, the English philosopher, describes problem solving in an interesting and picturesque way. He distinguishes among difficulties, puzzles, and problems. We solve a problem or make a discovery when we impose a puzzle form on a difficulty to convert it into a problem that can be solved in such a way that it gets us where we want to be. That is to say, we recast the difficulty into a form that we know how to work with—then we work it. Much of what we speak of as discovery consists of

[11] *Autobiography of Lincoln Steffens* (New York: Harcourt, Brace, 1931).

knowing how to impose a workable kind of form on various kinds of difficulties. A small but crucial part of discovery of the highest order is to invent and develop effective models or "puzzle forms." It is in this area that the truly powerful mind shines. But it is surprising to what degree perfectly ordinary people can, given the benefit of instruction, construct quite interesting and what, a century ago, would have been considered greatly original models.

Now to the hypothesis. It is my hunch that it is only through the exercise of problem solving and the effort of discovery that one learns the working heuristics of discovery; the more one has practice, the more likely one is to generalize what one has learned into a style of problem solving or inquiry that serves for any kind of task encountered—or almost any kind of task. I think the matter is self-evident, but what is unclear is the kinds of training and teaching that produce the best effects. How, for instance, do we teach a child to cut his losses but at the same time be persistent in trying out an idea; to risk forming an early hunch without at the same time formulating one so early and with so little evidence that he is stuck with it while he waits for appropriate evidence to materialize; to pose good testable guesses that are neither too brittle nor too sinuously incorrigible? And so on and on. Practice in inquiry, in trying to figure out things for oneself is indeed what is needed —but in what form? Of only one thing am I convinced: I have never seen anybody improve in the art and technique of inquiry by any means other than engaging in inquiry.

Conservation of memory. I have come to take what some psychologists might consider a rather drastic view of the memory process. It is a view that in large measure derives from the work of my colleague, George Miller.[12] Its first premise is that the principal problem of human memory is not storage but retrieval. In spite of the biological unlikeliness

[12] G. A. Miller, "The Magical Number Seven, Plus or Minus Two," *Psychological Review,* no. 63 (1956), pp. 81–97.

of it, we seem to be able to store a huge quantity of information—perhaps not a full tape recording, though at times it seems we even do that, but a great sufficiency of impressions. We may infer this from the fact that recognition, the ability to recall with maximum promptings, is so extraordinarily good in human beings and that spontaneous recall, with no promptings, is so extraordinarily bad. The key to retrieval is organization or, in even simpler terms, knowing where to find information that has been put into memory.

Let me illustrate with a simple experiment. We present pairs of words to twelve-year-olds. The children of one group are told only to remember the pairs and that they will be asked to repeat them later. Others are told to remember the pairs by producing a word or idea that will tie them together in a way that will make sense. The word pairs include such juxtapositions as "chair-forest," "sidewalk-square," and the like. One can distinguish three styles of mediators, and children can be scaled in terms of their relative preference for each: generic mediation, in which a pair is tied together by a superordinate idea: "chair and forest are both made of wood"; thematic mediation, in which the two terms are imbedded in a theme or a little story: "the lost child sat on a chair in the middle of the forest"; and part-whole mediation, in which "chairs are made from trees in the forest" is typical. Now the chief result, as you would predict, is that children who provide their own mediators do best—indeed, one time through a set of thirty pairs, they recover up to 95 percent of the second words when presented with the first ones of the pairs, whereas the uninstructed children reach a maximum of less than 50 percent recovered. Also, children do best in recovering materials tied together by the form of mediator they most often use.

One can cite a myriad of findings to indicate that any organization of information that reduces the aggregate complexity of material by imbedding it into a cognitive process a person has constructed for himself will make that material more accessible for retrieval. We may say that the process of memory, looked at from the retrieval side, is also a process of problem solving: how can material be "placed" in memory so that it can be obtained on demand?

We can take as a point of departure the example of the children who developed their own technique for relating each word pair. The children with the self-made mediators did better than the children who were given ready-made ones. Another group of children were given the mediators developed by this group to aid them in memorizing—a set of "ready-made" memory aids. In general, material that is organized in terms of a person's own interests and cognitive structures is material that has the best chance of being accessible in memory. It is more likely to be placed along routes that are connected to one's own ways of intellectual travel. Thus, the very attitudes and activities that characterize figuring out or discovering things for oneself also seem to have the effect of conserving memory.

On Learning Mathematics

I take as my starting point a notion of the philosopher Weldon, one I have mentioned before. He said that one can discriminate among difficulties, puzzles, and problems. A difficulty is a trouble with minimum definition. It is a state in which we know that we want to get from here to there, both points defined rather rawly and without much of an idea of how to bridge the gap. A puzzle, on the other hand, is a game in which there is a set of givens and a set of procedural constraints, all precisely stated. A puzzle also requires that we get from here to there, and there is at least one admissible route by which we can do so, but the choice of route is governed by definite rules that must not be violated. A typical puzzle is that of the Three Cannibals and Three Missionaries, in which you must get three missionaries and three cannibals across a river in a boat that carries no more than two passengers. You can never have more cannibals than missionaries on one side at a time. Only one cannibal can row; all three missionaries can. Now Weldon proposes, you recall, that a problem is a difficulty upon which we attempt to impose a puzzle form. A young man, trying to win the favor of a young lady—a difficulty—decides to try out successively, with benefit of correction by experience, a strategy of flattery—an iterative procedure and a classic puzzle—and thus converts his difficulty into a problem. I rather expect that most young men do all this deciding at the unconscious level. The point of mentioning it is to emphasize that the conversion of difficulties into problems by the imposition of puzzle forms is often not always done with cool awareness, and that part of the task of the mathematician is to work toward an increase in such awareness.

The pure mathematician is above all a close student of puzzle forms—puzzles involving the ordering of sets of elements in a manner to fulfill specifications. The puzzles, once grasped, are obvious, so obvious that it is astounding that anybody has difficulty with mathematics at all, as Bertrand Russell once said in exasperation. The answer to our puzzle is simple. The rowing cannibal takes over another cannibal and returns. Then he takes over the other cannibal and returns. Then two missionaries go over, and one of them brings back a nonrowing cannibal. Then a missionary takes the rowing cannibal over and brings back a nonrowing cannibal. Then two missionaries go over and stay, while the rowing cannibal travels back and forth, bringing the remaining cannibals over one at a time. And there are never more cannibals than missionaries on either side of the river. If you say that my statement of the solution is clumsy and lacking in generality, even though it is correct, you are quite right. But now we are talking mathematics.

For the mathematician's job is not pure puzzle mongering. It is to find the deepest properties of puzzles so that he may recognize that a particular puzzle is an examplar—trivial, degenerate, or important, as the case may be—of a family of puzzles. He is also a student of the kinship that exists among families of puzzles. So, for example, he sets forth such structural ideas as the commutative, associative, and distributive laws to show the manner in which a whole set of seemingly diverse problems have a common puzzle form imposed on them.

There probably are two ways in which one goes about both learning mathematics and teaching it. One of them is through a technique that I like to call unmasking, although it is sometimes called empirical generalization. Roughly, it consists in discovering or unmasking certain abstract properties that characterize solutions of more or less practical problems. Thus, the solving of surveying and triangulation problems in the ancient Nile valley, undertaken to reconstruct land boundaries after flooding, provided an empirical starting point for the development of abstract geometry and trigonometry. And so, too, in teaching we use "practical problems" or "concrete embodiments" to equip the learner with the experiences upon which later abstractions can be based. Such devices as the Cuisenaire rods, various of the block sets now on the market, and the "mathematical laboratory" are aids in this approach.

A second approach to mathematics teaching, which by no means excludes the first, is to work directly on the nature of puzzles themselves—on mathematics per se. If the first approach is somewhat semantic, going from things to the symbols used for characterizing them, then the second is principally syntactic in emphasis. For it is concerned not with what mathematical ideas and relations "stand for" or are "derived from" but rather with the grammar of mathematics as such. Empirical reference is put in a secondary position and, if one were to think of an example in teaching, the use of numbers to different bases than the base 10 is a nice one.

Obviously, both the working research mathematician and the person learning mathematics for the first time use both approaches in some optimum sequence.

In what follows, we shall be concerned with four aspects of the teaching or learning of mathematics. The first has to do with the role of *discovery* and if it is important or not that the learner discover things for himself. The second aspect is *intuition,* the class of nonrigorous ways by which mathematicians speed toward solutions or cul-de-sacs. The third is mathematics as an analytic language, and I shall concentrate on the problem of the *translation* of intuitive ideas into mathematics. This assumes that anything that can be said in mathematical form can also be said in ordinary language, though it may take a tediously long time to say it and there will always be the danger of imprecision of expression. The fourth and final problem is the matter of *readiness:* when is a child "ready" for geometry or topology or a discussion of truth tables?

Discovery. Much has already been said in the preceding essay about the act of discovery. The learning of mathematics provides a test case for some of the notions considered there. Take first the distinction between an active, manipulative approach to learning and the passive approach—the first likened to a speaker's decisions in using language and the second to a listener's. We do a disservice to our subject by calling the stimulation of active thinking, "the method of discovery." For there is certainly more than one method and each teacher has his own tricks for stimulating the quest in his pupils. Indeed, I am impressed by the fact that almost anything that gets away from the usual approach to natural numbers and their mechanical manipulation has the effect of freshening the student's taste for discovering things for himself. It would be better to consider how discovery usually proceeds when it does occur.

My own observation is that discovery in mathematics is a byproduct of making things simpler. Perhaps this is true of growth in pursuing other intellectual disciplines as well, but that is an issue that should not divert us, though a good case can be made for it, I think.[1] In any case, where mathematics is concerned, the issue hinges on *how* simplification occurs. It results most often from a succession of constructing representations of things. We do something that is manipulative at the outset—literally, provide a definition of something in terms of action. A hole is to dig, a yard is to pace off or apply a ruler to, subtraction is to take away. That is the start. But it is a start that provides the material for a second step. For having

[1] See J. S. Bruner and R. R. Olver, "The Growth of Equivalence Transformations in Children," *Child Development Monographs,* in press.

acted—paced off, taken away, turned upside down, or whatnot—
we are then able to turn around on our own actions and represent them. Having considered the ways of "saying-doing" how
big or long things are by pacing, putting fingers next to each
other, or using a ruler, we may simplify by characterizing all
these activities as measuring. In the effort to relate these
measuring actions one to the other, it is a very distracted child
who will not rediscover the importance of the unit of measure
as a means of getting all this welter of activity into a single,
simpler framework. Then and only then can there be fruitful
discussion of how we construct a unit of measure.

Learning to simplify is to climb on your own shoulders to
be able to look down at what you have just done—and then to
represent it to yourself. The constructing or doing that precedes the new representation can be well or poorly designed.
The good teacher is one who can construct exercises (or, better,
provide experiences) that cry for representation in the manner
that the one shoe dropped on the floor above cries to have the
second one drop. The poor teacher permits so much irrelevant
action to occur in such self-obscuring sequences that only a
genius could give a coherent account of what he had been up
to. Indeed, we can revise a refrain of an earlier chapter to
read, "How can I know what I think until I represent what
I do?"

Manipulation and representation, then, in continuing cycles
are necessary conditions for discovery. They are the antitheses
of passive, listenerlike learning. Yet representation is not
frenzied activity. Though active, it is still ratiocination, a
going back over experience, a listening to oneself. Nor should
we think that a teacher cannot play a role. Perhaps, in discussing the functions of teaching, we should make a special place
for the art of teaching people to listen to what they have been
doing so that their actions can be converted into representations of what they have done and what has resulted. If Percy
Bridgman's argument in his long effort to persuade scientists

to define their concepts in terms of the operations employed in arriving at them could be turned around to read backward, it would fit our case well. Our task as teachers is to lead students to develop concepts in order to make sense of the operations they have performed. Bridgman's dictum should, I think, be converted into a two-way street.

Intuition. It is particularly when I see a child going through the mechanical process of manipulating numbers without any intuitive sense of what it is all about that I recall the lines of Lewis Carroll: "Reeling and Writhing, of course, to begin with . . . and then the different branches of Arithmetic—Ambition, Distraction, Uglification, and Derision." Or as Max Beberman has put it, much more gently, "Somewhat related to the notion of discovery in teaching is our insistence that the student become aware of a concept before a name has been assigned to the concept." I am quite aware that the issue of intuitive understanding is a very live one among teachers of mathematics, and even a casual reading of the twenty-fourth *Yearbook* of the National Council of Teachers of Mathematics makes it clear that they are also very mindful of the gap that exists between proclaiming the importance of such understanding and actually producing it in the classroom.

Intuition implies the act of grasping the meaning or significance or structure of a problem without explicit reliance on the analytic apparatus of one's craft. It is the intuitive mode that yields hypotheses quickly, that produces interesting combinations of ideas before their worth is known. It precedes proof; indeed, it is what the techniques of analysis and proof are designed to test and check. It is founded on a kind of combinatorial playfulness that is only possible when the consequences of error are not overpowering or sinful. Above all, it is a form of activity that depends upon confidence in the worthwhileness of the process of mathematical activity rather than upon the importance of right answers at all times.

I shall examine briefly what intuition might be from a psychological point of view and consider what we can do about stimulating it among our students. Perhaps the first thing that can be said about intuition when applied to mathematics is that it involves the embodiment or concretization of an idea, not yet stated, in the form of some sort of operation or example. I watched a ten-year-old playing with snail shells he had gathered, putting them into rectangular arrays. He discovered that there were certain quantities that could not be put into such a rectangular compass, that however arranged there was always one left out. This of course intrigued him. He also found that two such odd-man-out arrays put together produced an array that was rectangular, that "the left-out ones could make a new corner." I am not sure it is fair to say that this child was learning much about prime numbers. But he most certainly was gaining the intuitive sense that would make it possible for him later to grasp what a prime number is and, indeed, what the structure of a multiplication table is.

I am inclined to think of mental development as involving the construction of a model of the world in the child's head, an internalized set of structures for representing the world around him. These structures are organized in terms of perfectly definite grammars or rules of their own, and in the course of development the structures change and the grammar that governs them also changes in certain systematic ways. The way in which we gain lead time for anticipating what will happen next and what to do about it is to spin our internal models just a bit faster than the world goes.

Now the child whose behavior I was just describing had a model of quantities and order that was implicitly governed by all sorts of seemingly subtle mathematical principles, many of them newly acquired and some of them rather strikingly original. He may not have been able to talk about them, but he was able to do all sorts of things on the basis of them. For example, he had "mastered" the very interesting idea of conservation of quantity across transformations in arrangement or, as you would say, the associative law. Thus, the quantity 6 can be stated as $2 + 2 + 2$, $3 + 3$, and by such "irregular" arrangements as $2 + 4$, $4 + 2$, $2 + (3 + 1)$, $(2 + 3) + 1$, and so on. Inherent in what he was doing was the concept of reversibility, as Piaget calls it, the idea of an operation and its inverse. The child was able to put two sets together and to take them apart; by putting together two prime-number arrays, he discovers that they are no longer prime (using our terms now) but can be made so again by separation. He was also capable of mapping one set uniquely on another, as in the construction of two identical sets. This is a formidable amount of highbrow mathematics.

Now what do we do with this rather bright child when he gets to school? In our own way we communicate to him that mathematics is a logical discipline and that it has certain rules, and we often proceed to teach him algorisms that make it seem that what he is doing in arithmetic has no bearing on the way in which he would proceed by nonrigorous means. I am not, mind you, objecting to "social arithmetic" with its interest rates and baseball averages. I am objecting to something far worse, the premature use of the language of mathematics, its end-product formalism, which makes it seem that mathematics is something new rather than something the child already knows. It is forcing the child into the inverse plight of the character in *Le Bourgeois Gentilhomme* who comes to the blazing insight that he has been speaking prose all his life. By interposing formalism, we prevent the child from realizing that he has been thinking mathematics all along. What we do, in essence, is to remove his confidence in his ability to perform the processes of mathematics. At our worst, we offer formal proof (which is necessary for checking) in place of direct intuition. It is good that a student knows how to check the conjecture that $8x$ is equivalent to the expression $3x + 5x$ by such a rigorous statement as the following: "By the commutative principle for multiplication, for every x, $3x + 5x = x3 + x5$.

By the distributive principle, for every x, $x3 + x5 = x(3 + 5)$. Again by the commutative principle, for every x, $x(3 + 5) = (3 + 5)x$ or $8x$. So, for every x, $3x + 5x = 8x$." But it is hopeless if the student gets the idea that this and this only is *really* arithmetic or algebra or "math" and that other ways of proceeding are really for nonmathematical dolts. Therefore, "mathematics is not for me."

It is important to allow the child to use his natural and intuitive ways of thinking, indeed to encourage him to do so, and to honor him when he does well. I cannot believe that he has to be taught this. Instead, we should first end our habit of inhibiting intuitive thinking and then find ways of helping the child improve at it.

Translation. The mathematician David Page wrote to me last year: "When I tell mathematicians that fourth-grade students can go a long way into 'set theory,' a few of them reply, 'Of course.' Most of them are startled. The latter are completely wrong in assuming that the set theory is intrinsically difficult. Of course, it may be that nothing is intrinsically difficult—we just have to wait the centuries until the proper point of view and corresponding language is revealed!" How can we state things in such a way that ideas can be understood and converted into mathematical expression?

It seems to me there are three problems here. Let me label them the problem of structure, the problem of sequence, and the problem of embodiment. When we try to get a child to understand a concept, leaving aside now the question of whether he can "say" it, the first and most important condition, obviously, is that the expositors themselves understand it. I make no apology for this necessary point. Its implications are not well understood. To understand something well is to sense wherein it is simple, wherein it is an instance of a simpler general case. I know that there are instances in the historical development of knowledge in which this may not be true, as in physics before Mendeleev's table or in contemporary physics where particle theory is for the moment seemingly moving toward divergence, rather than convergence, of principles. In the main, however, to understand something is to sense the simpler structure that underlies a range of instances, and this is notably true in mathematics.

In seeking to transmit our understanding of structure to another person, there is the problem of finding the language and ideas he would use if he were attempting to explain the same thing. If we are lucky, it may turn out that the language we would use would be within the grasp of the person we are teaching. When we are less fortunate, we are faced with the problem of finding a homologue that will contain our own idea moderately well and get it across without too much loss of precision—at least in a form that will permit us to communicate further at a later time.

For instance, we wish to tell the first-grade student that much of what we speak of as knowledge in science is indirect, that we talk about such things as pressure or chemical bonds or neural inhibition although we never encounter them direct-ly. They are inferences we draw from certain regularities in our observations. This is all very familiar to us. It is an idea with a simple structure but with complicated implications. It is difficult to tell the truth to a young student, used to thinking of things as either existing or not existing, who asks whether pressure "really" exists. We wish to transmit the idea that there are certain observations we make or operations we perform that turn out to be quite regular and predictable. We weigh things or study the manner in which our instruments move under set conditions. "Pressure" is the construct we invent to represent the operations we perform and the regularities in experience that occur when we perform them. Does pressure exist? Well, yes, provided you have invented it!

Now there is a sequence. How do we get the child to progress from his present two-value logic of things that exist and things that do not exist to a more subtle grasp of the matter? Take an example from the work of Inhelder and Piaget. They find that there are necessary sequences or steps in the mastery of a concept. In order for a child to understand the idea of serial ordering, he must first have a firm grasp of the idea of comparison—that one thing includes another or is larger than another. Or, in order for a child to grasp the idea that the angle of incidence is equal to the angle of reflection, he must first grasp the idea that for any angle at which a ball approaches a wall there is a corresponding unique angle by which it departs. Until he grasps this idea, there is no point in talking about the two angles being equal or bearing any particular relationship to each other, just as it is a waste to try to explain transitivity to a child who does not yet have a firm grasp on serial ordering.

The problem of embodiment then arises: how to embody illustratively the middle possibility of something that does not quite exist as a clear and observable datum? One group of chemists working on a new curriculum proposed as a transitional step in the sequence that the child be given a taped box containing an unidentified object. He may do anything he likes to the box: shake it, run wires through it, boil it, anything but open it. What does he make of it? I have no idea whether this gadget will get the child to the point where he can then more easily make the distinction between constructs and data. But the attempt is illustrative and interesting. It is a nice instance of how one seeks to translate a concept into a simpler form: that an object that cannot be seen can still be described—even if only indirectly. The object in this case "stands for" an invisible concept, albeit rather poorly, but it is a step in the right direction.

Surely all this argues for something akin to a spiral curriculum in which ideas are first presented in a form and language, honest though imprecise, which can be grasped by the child, ideas that can be revisited later with greater precision and power until, finally, the student has achieved the reward of mastery.[2]

Readiness. One of the conclusions of the 1959 Woods Hole Conference of the National Academy of Sciences on curriculum in science was that any subject can be taught to anybody at any age in some form that is honest. It is a brave assertion, and the evidence on the whole is all on its side. At least there is no evidence to contradict it.

Readiness, that is, is a function not so much of maturation as it is of our intentions and our skill at translating ideas into the language and concepts of the age level we are teaching. But our intentions must be plain before we can start deciding what can be taught to children of what age, for life is short and art is long and there is much art yet to be created in the transmission of knowledge. So a word about our intentions as educators.

When one sits down to the task of trying to write a textbook or to prepare a lesson plan, it soon becomes apparent that there is an antinomy between two ideals: coverage and depth. Perhaps this is less of a problem in mathematics than in the field of history or literature, but it is not by any means negligible. In content, positive knowledge is increasing at a rate that is alarming when considered in terms of what one man can know in a lifetime. But fortunately, as the bulk of knowledge increases, the organizing structures that support it also grow. So that if there is ever more knowledge, it may indeed be the case that it is ever more related: the only possible way in which individual knowledge can keep proportional pace with the surge of available knowledge is through a grasp of the relatedness of knowledge. We may well ask of any item of information that is taught or that we lead a child to discover for himself whether it is worth knowing. I can think of

[2] See J. S. Bruner, *The Process of Education* (Cambridge: Harvard University Press, 1960).

only two good criteria and one middling one for deciding such an issue: whether the knowledge gives a sense of delight and whether it bestows the gift of intellectual travel beyond the information given, in the sense of containing within it the basis of generalization. The middling criterion is whether the knowledge is useful. It turns out, on the whole, as Charles Sanders Peirce commented, that useful knowledge looks after itself. So I would urge that we as schoolmen let it do so and concentrate on the first two criteria. Delight and travel, then.

It seems to me that the implications of this conclusion are that we opt for depth and continuity in our teaching, rather than coverage, and that we re-examine afresh what it is that gives a sense of intellectual delight to a person who is learning. To do the first of these, we must ask what it is that we wish the man of our times to know, what sort of minimum. What do we mean by an educated man? I think that, at the very least, an educated man should have a sense of what knowledge is like in some field of inquiry, to know it in its connectedness and with a feeling for how the knowledge is gained. An educated man must not be dazzled by the myth that advanced knowledge is the result of wizardry. The way to battle this myth is in the direct experience of the learner—to give him the experience of going from a primitive and weak grasp of some subject to a stage in which he has a more refined and powerful grasp of it. I do not mean that each man should be carried to the frontiers of knowledge, but I do mean that it is possible to take him far enough so that he himself can see how far he has come and by what means.

The principles of conservation in physics, which are useful elsewhere in this book, are vividly illustrative here. I mean the conservation of energy, mass, and momentum; and I would include the idea of invariance across transformation in order to include mathematics more directly. The child is told, by virtue of living in our particular society and speaking our particular language, that he must not waste his energy, fritter it away. In common experience, things disappear, get lost. Bodies "lose" their heat; objects set in motion do not appear to stay in motion as in the pure case of Newton's law. Yet the most powerful laws of physics and chemistry are based on the conception of conservation. Only the meanest of purists would argue against the effort to teach the conservation principles to a first-grade student on the grounds that it would be "distorted" in the transmission. We know from the work of Piaget and others that, indeed, the child does not easily agree with notions based on conservation. A six-year-old child will often doubt that there is the same amount of fluid in a tall, thin glass jar as there was in a flat, wide one, even though he has seen the fluid poured from the latter into the former. Yet with time and with the proper embodiment of the idea—as in the film of the Physical Science Study Committee where a power plant is used as an example—it can be presented in its simplest and weakest form. The idea should be revisited constantly. It is central to the structure of the sciences of nature. In good time, many things can be derived from it that yield tremendous predictive power. Coverage in this sense, then, showing the range of things that can be related to this particular and powerful something, serves the ends of depth.

But what of delight? If you should ask me as a student of thought processes what produces the most fundamental form of pleasure in man's intellectual life, I think I would reply that it is the reduction of surprise and complexity to predictability and simplicity. But immediately there is a paradox. For it is the *act* of reducing surprise and complexity that gives pleasure. The road is better than the inn, for there is not all that much delight in simple unsurprisingness, and the cry "Not that *again!*" is surely a cry of dismay. It is precisely this readiness for new acts of simplification and surprise reduction that provides the thread of delight in what we have called a spiral curriculum. The great structural themes in learning lend themselves to just such an approach, to constant revisits yielding new discovery, new surprise and its reduction, new and deeper simplification.

My choice of the conservation theorems in physics as an illustration to be repeated has not been adventitious. It is as basic and ramifying in one's growing understanding of nature as any theme could be. There are similar themes in other fields: the idea of biological continuity in nature that begins, perhaps, with the observation that giraffes have giraffe babies and not little elephants and progresses eventually to the "memory" of the large helical molecules of DNA that bring the feat off; the associative, distributive, and commutative laws in mathematics; the elaboration of the concept of tragedy in literature.

When we are clear about what we want to do in this kind of teaching, I feel reasonably sure that we shall be able to deal with the pseudoproblem of readiness. We shall have to use the unfolding of readiness to our advantage: to give the child a sense of his own growth and his own capacity to leap ahead. The evidence shows that the problem of translating concepts to this or that age level can be solved once we decide what it is we want to translate.

After John Dewey, What?

 In 1897, at the age of thirty-eight, John Dewey published a stirring and prophetic work entitled *My Pedagogic Creed*. Much of his later writing on education is foreshadowed in this brief document. Five articles of faith are set forth. The first defines the educational process: "All education proceeds by the participation of the individual in the social consciousness of the race. This process begins unconsciously almost at birth, and is continually shaping the individual's powers, saturating his consciousness, forming his habits, training his ideas, and arousing his feelings and emotions."

The second article of faith embodies Dewey's concept of the school: "Education being a social process, the school is simply that form of community life in which all those agencies are concentrated that will be most effective in bringing the child to share in the inherited resources of the race, and to use his own powers for social ends. Education, therefore, is a process of living and not a preparation for future living." In the third thesis Dewey speaks to the subject matter of education: "The social life of the child is the basis of concentration or correlation in all his training or growth. The social life gives the unconscious unity and the background of all his efforts and all his attainments. . . . The true center . . . is not science, nor literature, nor history, nor geography, but the child's own social activities." A view of educational method gives form to Dewey's fourth article: "The law for presenting and treating material is the law implicit in the child's own nature." For Dewey, the law was that of action: "the active side precedes the passive in the development of the child-nature. I believe that consciousness is essentially motor or impulsive; that conscious states tend to project themselves in action." And, finally, Dewey's fifth thesis: "Education is the fundamental method of social progress and reform."

One reads the document today with mixed feelings. Its optimism is classically American in its rejection of the tragic view of life. It defines truth in the pragmatic spirit: truth is the fruit of inquiry into the consequences of action. It expresses a firm faith not only in the individual's capacity to grow but in society's capacity to shape man in its own best image. The final lines of the creed are these: "Every teacher should realize the dignity of his calling; that he is a social servant set apart for the maintenance of proper social order and the securing of the right social growth. In this way the teacher always is the prophet of the true God and the usherer in of the true kingdom of heaven."

Yet the very wholesomeness—the optimism, the pragmatism, the acceptance of man's harmonious continuity with society— leaves one uneasy. For in the two thirds of a century between 1897 and today, there has been a profound change not only in our conception of nature but also of society and the world of social institutions. Perhaps more important, we have lived through a revolution in our understanding of the nature of man, his intelligence, his capabilities, his passions, and the forms of his growth.

Dewey's thinking reflected the changes, though he was limited by the premises of his philosophical position. But between Dewey's first premises and our day, there bristles a series of revolutionary doctrines and cataclysmic events that change the very character of the inquiry. Two world wars, the dark episode of Hitler and genocide, the Russian revolution, the relativistic revolution in physics and psychology, the Age of Energy with its new technology, the sardonic reign of skeptical philosophy—all of these have forced a reappraisal of the underlying terms by which we construct a philosophy of education.

Let us then re-examine the terms, guided by what we know today of the world and of human nature. There is matter here, however, that is liable to some misinterpretation and we do well to clear it up at the outset. One writes against the background of one's day. Dewey was writing with an eye to the sterility and rigidity of school instruction in the 1890s—particularly its failure to appreciate the nature of the child. His emphasis upon the importance of direct experience and social action was an implied critique of the empty formalism that did little to relate learning to the child's world of experience. Dewey did mighty service in inspiring a correction. But an excess of virtue is vice. We, in our day, are reconsidering education against the background of such an excess.

Then, too, misunderstanding often converted Dewey's ideas into the sentimental practices he so deplored: "Next to deadness and dullness, formalism and routine," he wrote in his creed, "our education is threatened by no greater evil than sentimentalism." The sentimental cult of "the class project," of "life adjustment" courses, the reluctance to expose the child to the startling sweep of man and nature for fear it might violate the comfortable domain of his direct experience, the cloying concept of "readiness"—these are conceptions about children, often with no experimental support, that are justified in the name of Dewey. His was a noble yet tender view in his time. But what of our times? In what form shall we speak our beliefs?

What education is. Education seeks to develop the power and sensibility of mind. On the one hand, the educational process transmits to the individual some part of the accumulation of knowledge, style, and values that constitutes the culture of a people. In doing so, it shapes the impulses, the consciousness, and the way of life of the individual. But education must also seek to develop the processes of intelligence so that the individual is capable of going beyond the cultural ways of his social world, able to innovate in however modest a way so that he can create an interior culture of his own. For whatever the art, the science, the literature, the history, and the geography of a culture, each man must be his own artist, his own scientist, his own historian, his own navigator. No person is master of the whole culture; indeed, this is almost a defining characteristic of that form of social memory that we speak of as culture. Each man lives a fragment of it. To be whole, he must create his own version of the world, using that part of his cultural heritage he has made his own through education.

In our time, the requirements of technology constrain the freedom of the individual to create images of the world that are satisfying in the deepest sense. Our era has also witnessed the rise of ideologies that subordinate the individual to the defined aims of a society, a form of subordination that is without compassion for idiosyncracy and respects only the instrumental contribution of a man to the progress of the society. At the same time, and in spite of ideologies, man's understanding of himself and of his world—both the natural and social world— has deepened to a degree that warrants calling our age an intellectually golden one. The need is now to employ our deeper understanding not only for the enrichment of society but also for the enrichment of the individual.

It is true, as Dewey said, that all education proceeds by the participation of the individual in the social consciousness of the race, but it is a truth with a double edge. For all education, good and bad alike, is of this order. We know now to what degree this is so. To take but one example, the very language one speaks conditions the style and structure of thought and experience. Indeed, as we have seen, there is reason to believe that thought processes themselves are internalizations of social intercourse, an inner colloquy patterned by early external dialogues. It is this that makes education possible. But education, by giving shape and expression to our experience, can also be the principal instrument for setting limits on the enterprise of mind. The guarantee against limits is the sense of alternatives. Education must, then, be not only a process that transmits culture but also one that provides alternative views of the world and strengthens the will to explore them.

After a half century of startling progress in the psychological sciences, we know that mental health is only a minimum condition for the growth of mind. The tragedy of mental illness is that it so preoccupies the person with the need to fend off realities with which he cannot cope that it leaves him without either the nerve or the zest to learn. But mental health is only a state from which to start: the powers of mind grow with their exercise. Adjustment is too modest an ideal, if it is an ideal at all. Competence in the use of one's powers for the development of individually defined and socially relevant excellence is much more to the point. After a half century of Freud, we know that the freeing of instinct and inclination is not an end in itself but a way station along the road to competence. What is most prophetic for us about Freud in this second half of the century is not his battle against the fetters of rigid moralism, but his formula: "Where there was id, let there be ego."

Education must begin, as Dewey concluded his first article of belief, "with a psychological insight into the child's capacities, interests, habits," but a point of departure is not an itinerary. It is just as mistaken to sacrifice the adult to the child as to sacrifice the child to the adult. It is sentimentalism to assume that the teaching of life can be fitted always to the child's interests just as it is empty formalism to force the child to parrot the formulas of adult society. Interests can be created and stimulated. In this sphere it is not far from the truth to say that supply creates demand, that the provocation of what is available creates response. One seeks to equip the child with deeper, more gripping, and subtler ways of knowing the world and himself.

What the school is. The school is an entry into the life of the mind. It is, to be sure, life itself and not merely a preparation for living. But it is a special form of living, one carefully devised for making the most of those plastic years that characterize the development of *homo sapiens* and distinguish our species from all others. School should provide more than a continuity with the broader community or with everyday experience. It is primarily the special community where one experiences discovery by the use of intelligence, where one leaps into new and unimagined realms of experience, experience that is discontinuous with what went before. A child recognizes this when he first understands what a poem is, or what beauty and simplicity inhere in the idea of the conservation theorems, or that measure is universally applicable. If there is one continuity to be singled out, it is the slow converting of the child's artistic sense of the omnipotence of thought into the realistic confidence in the use of thought that characterizes the effective man.

In insisting upon the continuity of the school with the community on the one side and the family on the other, John Dewey overlooked the special function of education as an opener of new perspectives. If the school were merely a transition zone from the intimacy of the family to the life of the community, it would be a way of life easily enough arranged. In the educational systems of primitive societies, there almost always comes a point, usually at puberty, where there is a sharp change in the life of the boy, marked by a *rite de passage* that establishes a boundary between childhood ways and the ways of the adolescent.

It would be romantic nonsense to pattern our practices upon those found in preliterate societies. I would only ask that we attend to one parallel: education must not confuse the child with the adult and must recognize that the transition to adult-hood involves an introduction to new realms of experience, the discovery and exploration of new mysteries, the gaining of new powers.

In the *shtetl* of Eastern Europe, the traditional Jewish ghetto, the scholar was a particularly important figure—the *talmid khokhem*. In his mien, his mode of conversation so rich in allusion, his form of poise, the wise man was the image not of a competent but, rather, of a beautiful person. Traditional Chinese society also had its image of the beautiful person, one who blended knowledge and sentiment and action in a beauti-ful way of life. The ideal of the gentleman served much the same function in the Europe of the seventeenth and eighteenth centuries. It is perhaps in this spirit that Alfred North White-head declared that education must involve an exposure to greatness if it is to leave its mark. For me the yeast of educa-tion is the idea of excellence, and that comprises as many forms as there are individuals to develop a personal image of excel-lence. The school must have as one of its principal functions the nurturing of images of excellence.

A detached conception of idealized excellence is not enough. A doctrine of excellence, to be effective, must be translatable into the individual lives of those who come in contact with it. What is compelling about the *talmid khokhem,* the Chinese scholar-administrator, and the eighteenth-century gentleman is that they embody ways of life to which any man can aspire in his own way and from which he can draw in his own style. I believe, then, that the school must also contain men and women who, in their own way, seek and embody excellence. This does not mean that we shall have to staff our schools with men and women of great genius but that the teacher must embody in his own approach to learning a pursuit of excel-lence. And, indeed, with the technical resources opened by television and its adjuncts, one can present the student and also his teacher with the working version of excellence in its highest sense. In the years ahead, we shall find that the great scholar, scientist, or artist can speak as easily and honestly to the beginner as to the graduate student.

The subject matter of education. The issue of subject matter in education can be resolved only by reference to one's view of the nature of knowledge. Knowledge is a model we construct to give meaning and structure to regularities in experience. The organizing ideas of any body of knowledge are inventions for rendering experience economical and connected. We invent concepts such as force in physics, the bond in chemistry, motives in psychology, style in literature as means to the end of comprehension.

The history of culture is the history of the development of great organizing ideas, ideas that inevitably stem from deeper values and points of view about man and nature. The power of great organizing concepts is in large part that they permit us to understand and sometimes to predict or change the world in which we live. But their power lies also in the fact that ideas provide instruments for experience. Having grown up in a culture dominated by the ideas of Newton, and so with a conception of time flowing equably, we experience time moving inexorably and steadily, marked by a one-way arrow. Indeed, we know now, after a quarter of a century of research on perception, that experience is not to be had directly and neatly, but filtered through the programmed readiness of our senses. The program is constructed with our expectations and these are derived from our models or ideas about what exists and what follows what.

From this, two convictions follow. The first is that the structure of knowledge—its connectedness and the derivations that make one idea follow from another—is the proper emphasis in education. For it is structure, the great conceptual inventions that bring order to the congeries of disconnected observations, that gives meaning to what we may learn and makes possible the opening up of new realms of experience. The second conviction is that the unity of knowledge is to be found within knowledge itself, if the knowledge is worth mastering.

To attempt a justification of subject matter, as Dewey did, in terms of its relation to the child's social activities is to misunderstand what knowledge is and how it may be mastered. The significance of the concept of commutativity in mathematics does not derive from the social insight that two houses with fourteen people in each is not the same as fourteen houses with two people in each. Rather, it inheres in the power of the idea to create a way of thinking about number that is lithe and beautiful and immensely generative—an idea at least as powerful as, say, the future conditional tense in formal grammar. Without the idea of commutativity, algebra would be impossible. If set theory—now often the introductory section in newer curriculums in mathematics—had to be justified in terms of its relation to immediate experience and social life, it would not be worth teaching. Yet set theory lays a foundation for the understanding of order and number that could never be achieved with the social arithmetic of interest rates and bales of hay at so much per bale. Mathematics, like any other subject, must begin with experience, but progress toward abstraction and understanding requires precisely that there be a weaning away from the obviousness of superficial experience.

There is one consideration of cognitive economy, discussed in an earlier chapter, that is paramount. One cannot "cover" any subject in full, not even in a lifetime, if coverage means visiting all the facts and events and morsels. Subject matter presented so as to emphasize its structure will perforce be of that generative kind that permits reconstruction of the details or, at very least, prepares a place into which the details, when encountered, can be put.

What then of subject matter in the conventional sense? The answer to the question, "What shall be taught?" turns out to be the answer to the question, "What is nontrivial?" If one can first answer the question, "What is worth knowing about?"

then it is not difficult to distinguish between the aspects of it that are worth teaching and learning and those that are not. Surely, knowledge of the natural world, knowledge of the human condition, knowledge of the nature and dynamics of society, knowledge of the past so that it may be used in experiencing the present and aspiring to the future—all of these, it would seem reasonable to suppose, are essential to an educated man. To these must be added another: knowledge of the products of our artistic heritage that mark the history of our aesthetic wonder and delight.

A problem immediately arises concerning the symbolism in terms of which knowledge is understood and talked about. There is language in its natural sense and language in its mathematical sense. I cannot imagine an educated man a century from now who will not be largely bilingual in this special sense—concise and adept in both a natural language and mathematics. For these two are the tools essential to the unlocking of new experience and the gaining of new powers. As such, they must have a central place in any curriculum.

Finally, it is as true today as it was when Dewey wrote that one cannot foresee the world in which the child we educate will live. Informed powers of mind and a sense of potency in action are the only instruments we can give the child that will be invariable across the transformations of time and circumstance. The succession of studies that we give the child in the ideal school need be fixed in only one way: whatever is introduced, let it be pursued continuously enough to give the student a sense of the power of mind that comes from a deepening of understanding. It is this, rather than any form of extensive coverage, that matters most.

The nature of method. The process and the goal of education are one and the same thing. The goal of education is disciplined understanding; that is the process as well.

Let us recognize that the opposite of understanding is not ignorance or simply "not knowing." To understand something is, first, to give up some other way of conceiving of it. Confusion all too often lies between one way of conceiving and another, better way. It is one of our biological inheritances that confusion produces emergency anxiety, and with anxiety there come the defensive measures—flight, fright, or freezing— that are antithetical to the free and zestful use of mind. The binding fact of mental life in child and adult alike is that there is a limited capacity for processing information—our span, as it is called, can comprise six or seven unrelated items simultaneously. Go beyond that and there is overload, confusion, forgetting. As George Miller has put it, the principle of economy is to fill our seven mental-input slots with gold rather than dross. The degree to which material to be learned is put into structures by the learner will determine whether he is working with gold or dross.

For this reason, as well as for reasons already stated, it is essential that, before being exposed to a wide range of material on a topic, the child first have a general idea of how and where things fit. It is often the case that the development of the general idea comes from a first round of experience with concrete embodiments of ideas that are close to a child's life. The cycle of learning begins, then, with particulars and immediately moves toward abstraction. It comes to a temporary goal when the abstraction can then be used in grasping new particulars in the deeper way that abstraction permits.

Insofar as possible, a method of instruction should have the objective of leading the child to discover for himself. Telling children and then testing them on what they have been told inevitably has the effect of producing bench-bound learners whose motivation for learning is likely to be extrinsic to the task—pleasing the teacher, getting into college, artificially maintaining self-esteem. The virtues of encouraging discovery are of two kinds. In the first place, the child will make what he learns his own, will fit his discovery into the interior world of culture that he creates for himself. Equally important, discovery and the sense of confidence it provides is the proper reward for learning. It is a reward that, moreover, strengthens the very process that is at the heart of education—disciplined inquiry.

The child must be encouraged to get the full benefit from what he learns. This is not to say that he should be required to put it to immediate use in his daily life, though so much the better if he has the happy opportunity to do so. Rather, it is a way of honoring the connectedness of knowledge. Two facts and a relation joining them is and should be an invitation to generalize, to extrapolate, to make a tentative intuitive leap, even to build a tentative theory. The leap from mere learning to using what one has learned in thinking is an essential step in the use of the mind. Indeed, plausible guessing, the use of the heuristic hunch, the best employment of necessarily in-sufficient evidence—these are activities in which the child needs practice and guidance. They are among the great anti-dotes to passivity.

Most important of all, the educational process must be free of intellectual dishonesty and those forms of cheating that explain without providing understanding. I have expressed the conviction elsewhere that any subject can be taught to any-body at any age in some form that is honest. It is not honest to present a fifth-grade social-studies class with an image of town government as if it were a den of cub scouts presided over by a parent figure interpreting the charter—even if the image set forth does happen to mesh with the child's immediate social experience. A lie is still a lie—even if it sounds like familiar truth. Nor is it honest to present a sixth-grade science class with a garbled but concrete picture of the atom that is, in its way, as sweeteningly false as the suburban image of town government given them the year before. A dishonest image can only discourage the self-generating intellectual inquiry out of which real understanding grows.

The school and social progress. I believe that education is the fundamental method of social change. Revolutions themselves are no better and are often less good than the ideas they embody and the means invented for their application. Change is swifter in our times than ever before in human history and news of it is almost instantaneous. If we are to be serious in the belief that school must be life itself and not merely preparation for life, then school must reflect the changes through which we are living.

The first implication of this belief is that means must be found to feed back into our schools the ever deepening insights that are developed on the frontiers of knowledge. This is an obvious point in science and mathematics, and continuing efforts are now being instituted to assure that new, more powerful, and often simpler ways of understanding find their way back into the classrooms of our primary and secondary schools. But it is equally important to have this constant refreshment from fields other than the sciences—where the frontiers of knowledge are not always the universities and research laboratories but political and social life, the arts, literary endeavor, and the rapidly changing business and industrial community. Everywhere there is change, and with change we are learning.

I see the need for a new type of institution, a new conception in curriculum. What we have not had and what we are beginning to recognize as needed is something that is perhaps best called an "institute for curriculum studies"—not one of them, but many. Let it be the place where scholars, scientists, men of affairs, and artists come together with talented teachers continually to revise and refresh our curriculums. It is an activity that transcends the limits of any of our particular university faculties—be they faculties of education, arts and science, medicine, or engineering. We have been negligent in coming to a sense of the quickening change of life in our time and its implications for the educational process. We have not shared with our teachers the benefits of new discovery, new insight, new artistic triumph. Not only have we operated with the notion of the self-contained classroom but also with the idea of the self-contained school—and even the self-contained educational system.

The Nobel poet or the ambassador to the United Nations, the brilliant cellist or the perceptive playwright, the historian making use of the past or the sociologist seeking a pattern in the present—these men, like the student, are seeking understanding and mastery over new problems. They represent excellence at the frontiers of endeavor. If a sense of progress and change toward greater excellence is to illuminate our schools, there must be a constant return of their wisdom and effort to enliven and inform teacher and student alike. There is no difference in kind between the man at the frontier and the young student at his own frontier, each attempting to understand. Let the educational process be life itself as fully as we can make it.

PART III

the Idea of Action

The last three essays are concerned with the relation of thought and action: the first with the control of human behavior in a democratic society, the second with the impact of Freud on man's image of himself and his capacities, and the third with human effectiveness and its relation to the conception of fate in an age of science.

Action can be said to be determined by what a man knows, although I do not mean this in the rationalist's sense of calculus based on close reckoning of all alternatives. Rather, knowing has many faces and it is a linguistic pity that the word is a singular gerund. For we know in the light of many states, and it is man's fate that knowing in one light often precludes knowing in another at the same time—as in Niels Bohr's now-famous dictum that you cannot know somebody at the same time in the light of love and the light of justice. So we can say that, though action follows from what one knows, it is also the case that it never follows from *all* that one knows. Perhaps it is just as well, or else we should be in a persistent tetanus of indecision.

In any case, it would seem to me to follow from this principle that action can be understood in terms of the selective principle by which we use the knowledge available to us. It is for this reason that I have addressed the three remaining essays to the nature of the conceptions that underlie action in the modern world. Man does not respond to a world that exists for direct touching. Nor is he locked in a prison of his own subjectivity. Rather, he represents the world to himself and acts in behalf of or in reaction to his representations. The representations are products of his own spirit as it has been formed by living in a society with a language, myths, a history, and ways of doing things. It is with these difficult issues that the final essays are concerned.

All three were prepared in their first versions for special celebrations. "The Control of Human Behavior" was presented in New York at the twenty-fifth anniversary of the Graduate Faculty of the New School for Social Research—the famous "University in Exile." The Freud essay was given at a special convocation of the American Academy of Arts and Sciences to honor the retirements of Percy Bridgman and Phillip Frank. It was later printed in the *Partisan Review* (Summer 1956) and *American Psychologist* (September 1956). A version of this also appeared in *Daedalus* (Winter 1958). "Fate and the Possible" was given at the Centenary of Massachusetts Institute of Technology as part of a panel discussion called "How Has Science in the Last Century Changed Man's View of Himself?" Since the tone and content of this essay was naturally and in some measure determined by the other panelists, I should record that they were the physicist Robert Oppenheimer, the novelist Aldous Huxley, and the theologian Paul Tillich.

The Control of Human Behavior

The most characteristic and indeed the defining thing about human behavior, or any behavior, is that it is virtually never random, that it is under the control of systematic processes impinging from outside or initiated from inside the organism. In the deepest sense, then, human behavior is always controlled. Many of the sources of control over behavior are, of course, other human beings and the societies they construct. And frequently societies and groups of human beings seek to gain control over aspects of human behavior that were formerly under the power of non-social forces, or of social forces that are considered wrong or unhealthy or illegal. I shall refer to controls of this order as deliberate controls, and they are well illustrated by laws, regulations, and certain kinds of formal education. But there are also forms of social control necessary for the operation of a society that are *not* deliberate; indeed, many of these may not even be recognized as existing—such inconspicuous influences as guiding myths and values and the various forms of child-rearing. This aspect of control is often referred to by anthropologists as "covert culture." I prefer the expression "latent culture" to avoid the pejorative meaning of the word covert.

Given the nature of societies, it is frequently the case that deliberate forms of control bear a seemingly capricious relation to the latent ones. As Clyde Kluckhohn has suggested, deliberate controls may express the official aspirations of a culture, latent ones its practice. And one may also find instances in which the manifest effort at control is a guilt reaction against the informal or latent techniques of control—as in punitive legislation directed against illegitimate children. Finally, there are instances in which manifest and latent controls operate with admirable congruence, as in the accord between regulations and beliefs about compulsory education in the United States. To understand the control of human behavior, one must attend both to the manifest and the latent and to the manner of their interaction.

There are two approaches to the problem of control. One of them, the one that is least often a target for moral indignation, consists in seeking to control men by shaping their conception of the world in which they live. Once we have determined how men shall perceive and structure the world with which they have commerce, we can then safely leave their actions to them—in the sense that, if they believe themselves to be standing before a precipice, they will not step over it unless they intend suicide. This is cognitive control, controlling men's minds, to use that pompous phrase. Achieving such control is exceedingly difficult—or, rather, usurping it is difficult, for the control now rests in the culture and its ways of introducing members into its web of reality.

The second approach is more direct in the sense that it does not seek directly to alter the experience of the person, but only his acts. It utilizes punishments and rewards: when the former are the chief instruments it is called coercion; with the latter it is seduction. There is a great deal that is moot on the subject of what combination of coercion and seduction is most effective in controlling behavior and whether, once having controlled overt acts, one thereby changes the person's view of what the reality was to which he had reacted. A growing body of data points to the conclusion that people act themselves into a way of believing as readily as they believe themselves into a way of acting. More simply, there is a strong human tendency toward construing one's acts as following from the reality of one's experience. Whether for reasons of cognitive economy or for the protection of self-esteem, people wish to see their acts as derived from, or congruent with, experience. The liking for absurdity is an acquired taste, and not widely distributed.

The distinction between cognitive control and control by coercion and seduction is a deep one. The one operates by intrinsic "self-administered" rewards and punishments; the other is regulated by gains and losses that are extrinsically administered. The distinction is familiar from its use in our earlier discussion of the act of discovery and in considering how one might fashion an ideal educational sequence. It is no exaggeration to say that the role given to each of these forms of control is a hallmark of any political theory of the state, and, by the same token, it is the single most telling feature of any psychological theory about the nature of man—whether one envisions man as ultimately captive of the shaping forces of his environment or as competent to shape a world of his own. It is an absorbing fact that psychological theory both in America and in the Soviet Union is sharply divided on this issue.[1]

There are certain generalizations one can make about the degree to which controls of all kinds can be made effective. Most of them are rather cheerful from the point of view of a pluralistic conception of democracy; none of them is particularly happy from the point of view of improving the conduct of man to make him a better citizen of a democracy. Two of these generalizations, the concept of monopolistic pre-emption and the concept of primacy, are closely related and worth considering here.

The concept of monopolistic pre-emption can be stated as follows. To the degree that one has monopolistic control of the

---

[1] See Raymond A. Bauer, *The New Man in Soviet Psychology* (Cambridge: Harvard University Press, 1952), and also my preface to L. Vygotsky's classic, *Thought and Language* (New York: John Wiley-Technology Press, 1962).

sources of information to which an individual is exposed and control over the order in which he encounters information, to that degree does one's opportunity for cognitive control increase. Similarly, in the realm of action, it follows that a monopoly over the means of coercion and seduction increases the potentiality for controlling human behavior. But just as the nature and order of information encountered must be manipulable to achieve cognitive control, so with coercion and seduction one must be able to reward or punish very quickly. If we know anything from the studies of the reinforcement of behavior in animals, it is that reward and punishment (but particularly the former) lose their power at a very sharp rate the further they are separated in time from the acts that they are supposed to be controlling. But we lose sight of the utopian conditions for all this—that *if* we had such monopolistic control, then we would be in good position to *attempt* to exercise control. It is not surprising that writers who are fond of fantasies about social control, like my colleague B. F. Skinner in his novel *Walden Two*, encourage themselves with tales set in a neatly arranged, benign, but nonetheless utterly monopolistic utopia.

A word now about primacy. Within interesting limits of error, it can be said that conceptions of reality early established tend to become the first editions of reality upon which later editions are fashioned. Though the later editions may change, they have a continuity or oppositional congruence with the earlier ones. In another place, I have written about the distinction between "line" and "filler" sources that people use in gaining information in an effort to maintain or modify their attitudes and values.[2] The filler sources may be found anywhere; line sources provide direct support to the more deeply selective principle in the person's approach to social reality. It is more often than not the case that the early versions of social

[2] See M. B. Smith, J. S. Bruner, and R. W. White, *Opinions and Personality* (New York: John Wiley, 1956).

reality have a pre-emptive power that makes them like line sources. I am not suggesting that people do not change their opinions and perspective on reality, but only that change always requires a reference point and that even violent change bears the mark of what was before. The passion of the ex-Communist become anti-Communist is all too familiar. Early emotionally organized beliefs and guides to action often may be stubbornly incorrigible, partly because they are isolated from the language-bound literal structure of reality that develops later. Such beliefs are hard to reach by the discourse of ordinary reason. It is thanks to one of Freud's great insights that psychoanalytic procedure can now bring some of them back into awareness where they can be linked to the day life of the ego. But psychoanalysis is for the few, and the ugly beast of Hitler, that if he could have the first dozen years of a child's life it mattered little who had the next twenty, still has nightmare quality.

One can go on almost endlessly speaking of the psychology of control without much reference to its implementation in society—talking as if the application of monopoly and primacy were simply matters of detail to be worked out later. Such a path deserves to be labeled *psychologist's fallacy*. It is the kind of misconception that leads some psychiatrists to argue that, if the hostility level of the man in the street could be lowered or diverted into other channels, there would be no war. It fails utterly to take into account the reality and complexity of social organization. It refuses to envisage the kind of social organization that would permit the impositions of those manifest and latent controls we know to be necessary if behavior is to be regulated. The fact of the matter is that only the most highly organized and ruthless totalitarian states ever consider the possibility of tackling the task. And they do so because they have a morality of government consonant with the administrative arrangements required. We do not. Although it is psychologically simpler and more spectacular to talk about such totalitarian forms of control as brainwashing and the measured use of terror, it is more useful to consider the matter of behaviorial control as it actually exists in limited form in democratic societies.

The first thing that can be said about the ethics and the techniques of control in a democracy is that both of them rest heavily upon certain cultural values concerning the nature of the private sphere: there are sharp differences between the theory of control as exercised over the public sphere of life and the private. The public sphere is governed by codes of law and regulatory legislation, backed by police power and the force of public opinion, and adjudicated either by courts of law or regulatory commissions. It is quite plain that practices in the public sphere depend upon and change with the corpus of beliefs and opinions that develop as expressions of private morality. And where there is a conflict between the two domains, public and private, it is an occasion for crisis within a society. Two such crises beset us today, both matters of sharp concern in the United States and Great Britain where each is approached quite differently. One has to do with capital punishment and its justification either as a legitimate expression of moral indignation or as a presumably rational concern for deterring crimes of violence. Both justifications collide with a Christianized private ideal of compassion and rehabilitation. The other crisis is the view of homosexuality as crime, an issue recently given an airing by the Royal Commission under Lord Wolfenden. In both cases it can be shown that the body of laws and their spirit as interpreted by the courts have influenced private morality. But whereas control is exercised in the public realm by instruments of government, the case is usually quite different in matters of private belief and action. Here one may speak of the instruments of a culture as decisive. What are these instruments?

A short list would include: language and myth, affiliative pressure, anticipation of rejection and isolation, limitation of opportunity, and variable compensation. Consider each of these in turn, and consider how each relates to monopoly and primacy.

Language and myth. It is perhaps Ernst Cassirer and Benjamin Lee Whorf who have made us most aware in recent times of the importance of myth and language in the shaping of man's conception of reality and of their consequent importance in the control of human behavior. Language and myth exercise this power by virtue of two circumstances—the first is the need to maintain communication because of the fractional competence of each individual in a society; the second is the requirement of conserving one's limited cognitive capacity. Myth and language each operate to accomplish both of these, and they maintain their controlling power because of their success. We have already considered the role of myth and language in shaping reality, but here a few words are needed to consider them as instruments of control.

Language is the human gift that is the chief guarantor of joint action, and it comes into its first use at a time when joint action is the only means whereby the young human organism can survive. Consequently, early language is essentially demand language, a two-way demand language. But language learning is also concept learning, and the price one pays for the gift of language is that one also learns to operate in terms of the concepts that are codified in a language—all the concepts of relationship, of modification, of cause and effect. I am not supporting the so-called strong form of Whorf's hypothesis— that language ineluctably molds the shape of thought—but rather the weaker form which holds that language predisposes a mind to certain modes of thought and certain ways of arranging the shared subjective reality of a linguistic community.

It is probably true that, given sufficient freedom of periphrasis, one can express any idea in any language, but the fact of the matter is that one usually does not. It is this cognitively predisposing property of a language that has been called its

Weltanschauung. Also, languages differ in their capacity to absorb and facilitate the use of new ideas that are not built-in features of a particular language. For example, Western languages may eventually absorb the idea of aspiration in a new structure of future tenses, adding to the future tense and the future conditional new forms that express the desired future state and the undesired one: on balance it will rain tomorrow, it could rain tomorrow, it should rain tomorrow, hopefully it will rain tomorrow, alas it will rain tomorrow. Our language absorbs such distinction easily. If Florence Kluckhohn is right in her claim that we are increasingly a "becoming" culture rather than a "being" one, then we are likely to develop such rules either formally or informally as a means of alerting the sensitivities of those who live in our culture. Perhaps we have already. The result in increased awareness represents a powerful form of control over reality.

Obviously, language and myth also play an enormous part, as we have already seen, in the conservation of cognitive capacity. What better way of coding and recoding experience than to catch its complexities in the constraining structure of words? As the social environment becomes increasingly complex, it becomes all the more important to have the words and concepts that can encompass the events and controls that we bring into being. We learn to segment the flow of events into "campaigns" or "crises" or "historical trends." Of course, a single participant in a linguistic community uses all the forms of regrouping experience that the culture provides. But there exists a linguistic and conceptual consensus that makes swift and widespread communication possible—and it is this consensus that provides yet another basis for the control of behavior, control in the sense that the result is a reduction in the variability of behavior.

And, to be sure, it is not only language and its concepts that operate in this fashion, but the myths and models provided by the society as well. A friend, a distinguished aeronautical engineer, recently told me of his visit to the Soviet Union during which a gifted Russian colleague pressed him for details of his personal finances as a professor in a great American university. My friend, after carefully telling about his salary and his consulting fees, then went on to talk about his taxes each year. The Russian, a highly intelligent man, immediately seized upon this detail and exclaimed, "But under socialism, we have no taxes." "Come now," said my friend, "how do you pay for your space program, your armed forces, your beautiful subways?" The Russian, a thoughtful man, was visibly disturbed by the question. It had penetrated.

The question of mythmaking as a technique of control can be more sharply put. I have argued earlier that in our time the intellectual can reclaim his powerful position as mythmaker; that the scientist and humanist between them can offer new images of man's place in the universe we are coming to know. Friendly critics of widely different training have complained that I have failed to see the organic, unconscious nature of the growth of myth to which, so goes the claim, the intellectual only gives words and a voice. I think the point is a moot one. Indeed, there is evidence that even enduring folk art is almost always of minority origin, that it was first created by one man for a small audience. The impact of the intellectual and the technician on the magical conception of juju in West Africa is more than just amusing. A Nigerian educator told me of one change in his native village over the past fifteen or twenty years. Then, the children would take to the bush when the "injection man" appeared with small-pox vaccines. Today, the villagers line up for inoculations performed by uneducated Africans who inject distilled water, sold for a guinea a shot, as "white man's juju."

Nobody would doubt that the intellectual, by virtue of his sensitivity to the inappropriateness of existing myths, has played a great role as myth slayer. Perhaps his role in the years ahead will be considerably more positive.

Affiliation and rejection. Margaret Mead some years ago drew a distinction among forms of public opinion. Some are controlled ritualistically, as in Balinese society where issues are said to be settled by deriving a solution from a ritualized code. Others are managed affiliatively, where the decision depends upon the group membership and relationship of the contending parties, as among the Iatmul. And there might be still others, where resolution depends on individual values, in which opinion crystallizes spontaneously. It is not easy to pick a society where this occurs, though we like to think of our own in these terms. In any case, we have seen how language and myth operate as powerful ritualistic controls even if they are not readily manageable. A brief look at affiliation and the fear of losing it will, I believe, disclose a powerful controlling force and one much more easily manipulated.

A useful point of departure is the interesting literature now available on separation trauma in children. From the work of John Bowlby and others, it appears that quite early in life there is an important period in which the child develops a strong love-dependency relationship with a parental figure who looks after the child and supplies care and continuity—and the two together are critical. Brief separation from the parent figure produces a marked upset; somewhat longer separation leads to what appears to be a denial reaction in which the parent is not recognized after return from, say, the hospital. Continued separation with inadequate subsitution of another parent figure leads to certain irreversible changes that, in adulthood and adolescence, become what is best summarized as psychopathy. It consists of an inability to form identifications with people, to commit oneself for long periods to a line of work or an enterprise. People who have been subjected to such treatment (as in the aseptic nurseries for orphans in the twenties that operated on the misguided belief that too much love is not good for children and that they should not be comforted when they cry or allowed to become attached to one nurse) characteristically slide into a "spiv" pattern, into petty thievery or casual prostitution, and they show various other forms of psychopathic drift through the demilegal borderlands of society. In short, they are hard to control by means other than confinement and coercion.

For the great majority who succeed in establishing affiliative identification with family, village, and society at large, there is a built-in vulnerability to control: the fear of ostracism. So far as I know, there is no society in which such isolation is not a source of dread. Perhaps, indeed, it is as widespread as the incest taboo.

Control of identification and manipulation of the threat of ostracism are the two great instruments by which human behavior is controlled by those who exert power—first in the family and later in the larger groups into which the person moves. It is central not only in the control of a democratic society but also in the totalitarian state. The renunciation of parental identification that is so much a part of the intense political schooling of China is not designed to destroy the capacity for identification but to transfer it to other symbols.

I have sometimes thought that we may have exaggerated the effects of childrearing practices on the adult personality as a general matter, but it has never crossed my mind that we have exaggerated the importance of identification in the childrearing process. Between the childrearing practices of one culture and another there is much in common that is dictated by the very nature of the task, whether in Detroit, in Peiping, or in Bali, and we have at times overlooked these communalities. But certainly it is clear that the capacity for identification, its quality, the transferability of identification, and the vividness and nature of the dread of isolation—all of these can be varied in striking ways by the handling of early dependency relationships.

What I should like to propose at this point is not that we seek to manipulate patterns of child training for achieving official forms of control over man's behavior. Rather, it is here that I would look for defense against controls of a kind that are likely to be dangerous to the future of a democratic society. Whoever is sick with the fear of rejection, whoever has formed too strong and transferable an identification—he is the potential victim of forms of control that make men unfree. If public-health measures are understood in their most profound sense as expressions of a society's values, then surely here is a prime area for taking measures to ensure the survival of democracy.

Limitation of opportunity. Again it is some recent work on early deprivation that gives a new meaning to the limitation of opportunity as a technique for controlling human behavior.[3] Specifically, the work concerns sensory deprivation, and the subjects were animals, mostly dogs. (It is not possible to do the equivalent experiments on human beings.) Raising a dog in a highly impoverished environment, where there is little variety and no challenge to problem solving, produces a seemingly irreversible stupidity in the adult animal. The puppy who has been isolated needs many trials before he learns not to sniff the candle flame that burns his nose as a price for his curiosity. He is very deficient in learning how to go around a barrier to get food on the other side, and in general his behavior is lacking in variety and flexibility.

Relatively little is known as yet about the rehabilitation of such animals, save that it is a very slow process. Again, there seems to be a critical period during which isolation from the world of rich stimulation has its maximum deleterious effect— during the first year principally. But there is evidence that there are effects, more or less irreversible, that are produced by prolonged exposure to dulled and homogenized environments during the formative years of any mammal. My children have raised rats from the Wistar Institute in the usual chaos of a human habitat and these rats were considerably more

[3] See Philip Solomon and others, eds., *Sensory Deprivation* (Cambridge: Harvard University Press, 1961).

exploratory, venturesome, and intelligent personalities than the rats who lived in the gray atmosphere of the laboratory. Reviewing the literature in early sensory deprivation, I have come to the conclusion that one of the chief effects of such restriction is that, to put it metaphorically, the animals are prevented from developing adequate models of the environment in which they will eventually have to live—or, technically stated, there is interference with the formation of what Hebb has called cell assemblies and phase sequences, the hypothetical neural structures that are constructed in our brains to represent and abstract the texture of the environment.

The reader may properly wonder at this point whether I am proposing that such forms of deprivation be used for controlling behavior in the spirit, say, that Huxley's planners in *Brave New World* produced "gammas." On the contrary, I am suggesting that we are already inadvertently controlling behavior by imposing irreversible limits upon it with many of our practices in education, considering education now in the broad sense. We should be asking whether there are critical periods for the introduction of training in mathematics and language and guiding myths. There probably are. Are we mindful of what it takes by way of intensive exposure to certain forms of experience to unlock human capacities of certain kinds, whether for looking at art or for manipulating abstract symbols? I rather think we are not.

A final psychological point about limitation of exposure. Many students of human development have noted that there is a phenomenon by which supply creates demand. Gordon Allport has written of the functional autonomy of motives, the sequence whereby a habitual activity seems to acquire a motive of its own for its continuation. Karl Bühler, commenting on the development of language in children, has, you will recall, proposed the concept of *Funktionslust*—pleasure derived from the exercise of a newly developed function or skill. Donald Hebb and Robert White (whose views we visited in an earlier essay) more recently have suggested that there seems to be an intrinsic pleasure or self-reward in gaining competence that feeds upon itself in the sense that the development of taste leads to increasing development of taste. How important this is in cultivating a taste for discovering we have already seen. It may well be that early sensory and intellectual deprivation prevents the kind of intellectual and emotional unfolding that nourishes early learning and makes later learning possible.

Compensation schedules. Finally, there is the thorny question of whether pay and its withholding is much of an instrument for the control of human behavior. For a psychologist this is unfamilar ground except insofar as rewards and punishments meted out in the training of laboratory animals and laboratory humans (by which I mean human beings made to respond in situations designed for animal response) are analogous to monetary or other forms of compensation and discipline. It is certainly plain that people can be paid for doing things, threatened with punishment if they do not do them, bribed, lured, or seduced by material rewards. Pay people adequately and reduce the noxious features of their work situation to a certain minimum and, in the main, they will do the job you hire them to do. A huge amount of the world's behavior is undoubtedly controlled in this way, notably in Western society. It constitutes a contractual arrangement where, in exchange for money or goods or prestige, an individual will sell to you the right to control his behavior within certain limits and for certain hours during a day. On the whole the system appears to work adequately.

This is all very well and may be just what it seems, but the startling thing to a psychologist is that the universal efficacy of the system is accepted so largely as a matter of faith. Not long ago I talked with the executive who designed and administers the compensation plan for an American corporation that hires about a third of a million employees. The company in question is enlightened, pays well, and gives large incentives to its workers and managers to shoot high. But the conversation was oddly disillusioning. What struck me and what the executive openly confessed worry over was the lack of any systematic work on the extent to which money and other kinds of pay form a satisfying compensation for individual workers—what economists speak of as the utility function for the forms of pay. This particular company operates on the principle that for all supervisory personnel within any given level there should be a wide range in salary, an "incentive" range of at least 35 percent above the base rate. I asked the theory behind it and, while I was given an interesting rule-of-thumb answer, it was not one based on a study of what increases in compensation do for productivity or human satisfaction. I have mentioned compensation rates as a problem here largely because such a universal form of controlling behavior should be better understood from the psychological point of view. Economics, like any other field in the social sciences, is too important to leave entirely to its own practitioners.

All of which is not to say that compensation is not one of the great controlling factors in modern life. Rather, what strikes me is that once one is above some sort of minimum subsistence level—as all affluent societies are—the meaning of compensation ceases to have an "economic" significance in a narrow sense and takes on a symbolic significance in the broadest and haziest sense. In America, if one should ask a cross-section of workers whether they are earning enough money, most of them would look at the interrogator incredulously. Of course not. Yet we do not understand what the threshold of satisfaction in pay is, expressed in monetary terms.

Let me suggest, partly in a playful spirit, that we would do well to add a theorem to our list of theorems having to do with the economics of compensation. It is derived from a point made earlier, that supply creates demand. It might go something like this: above the subsistence level, you do not need anything until you have it. That is to say, the anticipated value of money is not symmetrical with the value attached to the same amount of money once possessed and then lost. If one can say this for money, it can be said equally well for commodities or activities.

The theorem is based on the observation that to be deprived of an activity or of a habitual item of consumption is more disruptive of behavior than merely to want an activity or a thing that one has not had. We want any number of things and adjust with humor to our wants. But remove or diminish something around which we have organized a pattern of life, and a massive defense reaction is put into being.

Why should this be so psychologically? I think we have come upon part of the answer in what has already been discussed. Loss or reduction of compensation symbolizes withdrawal of support, a form of ostracism. So too with the symbolism of not being rewarded by raises at the same rate as those who appear to be doing the same work as you do. The traditional bitterness of the passed-over captain in our Navy is no exception. But beyond the symbolic spread of loss and reduction in compensation, there is one other powerful factor that operates. It is the stabilizing and simplifying role of expectation and habit in our daily lives—a subject about which William James wrote so brilliantly in his famous chapter on "Habit." Allport's doctrine of the functional autonomy of motives points in the same direction.

The implications of our hypothesis, and it should of course be treated as a very tentative one, is that economic affluence creates the condition for the use of compensation as a technique of blackmail—a most abhorrent conclusion. If indeed it is the case that the power of a system of compensation is the withdrawal of support from those who have become used to support, then the instrument of compensation (or, better, decompensation) is a powerful weapon for exacting compliance.

The great corporation of which we spoke, with its system of maintaining high variability from a base rate in paying its executives, is famous for the tensions and ulcers among them—and also for their efficiency. The techniques for beneficent blackmail, defined in terms of company objectives, are well built in. Money rewards (taken in the broadest sense) do not very likely operate as a simple utility function with effort or efficiency increasing as a function of increments in pay. A great deal of human behavior is indeed controlled by the contractual arrangement of wages, with services performed for money. But, in fact, the money or goods involved do not in themselves seem to do much by way of controlling the behavior. Rather, the nature of the job itself appears to provide the pattern of control. One gets a job as a mailman and one "behaves mailman," or if one is hired as a professor, one behaves that way. In time one develops what the French have long called *une déformation professionnelle,* a set of habits and outlooks to match the requirements of the job. One also develops an expectancy of support. To assure that the behaving is "professor" or "mailman" we use the coercive technique of withdrawal or reduction in support.

I would end with a conjecture about the control of human behavior. A colleague and friend has for some years been studying the social psychology of flattery. He distinguishes between normative and exploitative flattery—the former being the usual good manners involved in praising worthy efforts, the latter being perhaps too familiar to need much definition. He remarks that one of the costs of seeking to control others by flattery is that you forfeit an enormous amount of freedom in your own activity—who is controlled more by the flattery cycle, the flatterer or the flattered? So it is with control generally. The garrison state, the totalitarian state, the coercive institution all have it in common that they forfeit enormous resources to the maintenance of control. We have been concerned with control in a democratic society. The guiding rule in such societies cannot be how to obtain maximum or even optimum control of human behavior, including now the most heinous forms of behavior. Rather, the question is how one obtains the necessary control while preserving the necessary variability that permits change, innovation, zest, and a lively sense that the invention of new alternatives is more important than the suppression of ones that may prove ugly.

Freud and the Image of Man

 By the dawn of the sixth century before Christ, the Greek physicist-philosophers had formulated a bold conception of the physical world as a unitary material phenomenon. The Ionics had set forth a conception of matter as fundamental substance, transformation of which accounted for the myriad forms and substances of the physical world. Anaximander was subtle enough to recognize that matter must be viewed as a generalized substance, free of any particular sensuous properties. Air, iron, water, or bone were only elaborated forms, derived from a more general stuff. Since that time, the phenomena of the physical world have been conceived as continuous and monistic, as governed by the common laws of matter. The view was a bold one, bold in that it ran counter to the immediate testimony of the senses. It has served as an axiomatic basis of physics for more than two millennia. The bold view eventually became the obvious view, and it gave shape to our common understanding of the physical world. Even the alchemists rested their case upon this doctrine of material continuity and, indeed, they might even have hit upon the proper philosopher's stone.

The good fortune of the physicist—and these matters are always relative, for the material monism of physics may have impeded nineteenth-century thinking and delayed insights into the nature of complementarity in modern physical theory—this early good fortune or happy insight has no counterpart in the sciences of man. Lawful continuity between man and the animal kingdom, between dreams and unreason on one side and waking rationality on the other, between madness and sanity, between consciousness and unconsciousness, between primitive and civilized man—each of these has been a cherished discontinuity preserved in doctrinal canons. There were voices in each generation, to be sure, urging the exploration of continuities. Anaximander had a passing good approximation to a theory of evolution based on natural selection; Cornelius Agrippa offered a plausible theory of the continuity of mental health and disease in terms of bottled-up sexuality. But Anaximander did not prevail against Greek conceptions of man's creation nor did Cornelius Agrippa against the demonopathy of the *Malleus Maleficarum.* Neither in establishing the continuity between the varied states of man nor in pursuing the continuity between man and animal was there conspicuous success until the nineteenth century.

I need not insist upon the social, ethical, and political significance of this image, for it is patent that the view one takes of man affects profoundly one's standard of what is humanly possible. And it is by the measure of such a standard that we establish our laws, set our aspirations for learning, and judge the fitness of men's acts. It is no surprise, then, that those who govern must perforce be jealous guardians of man's ideas about man, for the structure of government rests upon an uneasy consensus about human nature and human wants. The idea of man is of the order of *res publica,* and, by virtue of its public status, it is an idea that is not subject to change without public debate. The behavioral scientist, as some insist on calling him, may propose, but it is the society at large that disposes. Nor is it simply a matter of public concern. For man as individual has a deep and emotional investment in his image of himself. If we have learned anything in the last half century of psychology, it is that man has powerful and exquisite capacities for defending himself against violations of his cherished self-image. This is not to say that Western man has not persistently asked: "What is man that thou art mindful of him?" It is only that the question, when pressed, brings us to the edge of anxiety where inquiry is no longer free.

Two figures stand out massively as the architects of our present-day conception of man: Darwin and Freud. Freud's was the more daring, the more revolutionary, and, in a deep sense, the more poetic insight. But Freud is inconceivable without Darwin.

Rear-guard fundamentalism did not require a Darwin to slay it in an age of technology. He helped, but this contribution was trivial in comparison with another. What Darwin did was to propose a set of principles unified around the conception that all organic species had their origins and took their form from a common set of circumstances—the requirements of biological survival. All living creatures were on a common footing. When the post-Darwin era of exaggeration had passed and religious literalism had abated into a new nominalism, what remained was a broad, orderly, and unitary conception of organic nature, a vast continuity from the monocellular protozoans to man. Biology had at last found its unifying principle in the doctrine of evolution. Man was not unique but the inheritor of an organic legacy.

As the summit of an evolutionary process, man could still view himself with smug satisfaction, indeed proclaim that God or Nature had shown a persistent wisdom in its effort to produce a final, perfect product. It remained for Freud to present the image of man as the unfinished product of nature: struggling against unreason, impelled by driving inner vicissitudes and urges that had to be contained if man were to live in society, host alike to seeds of madness and majesty, never fully free from an infancy that was anything but innocent.

What Freud was proposing was that man at best and at worst is subject to a common set of explanations: good and evil grow from a common process.

Freud was strangely yet appropriately fitted for his role as architect of a new conception of man. His qualifications are worth examining, for the image of man that he created was in no small measure founded on his painfully achieved image of himself and of his times. We are concerned not so much with his psychodynamics as with the intellectual traditions he embodies. A child of his century's materialism, he was wedded to the determinism and the classical physicalism of nineteenth-century physiology so boldly represented by Helmholtz. Indeed, the young Freud's devotion to the exploration of anatomical structures was a measure of the strength of this inheritance. But at the same time, as both Lionel Trilling and W. H. Auden have recognized with such sensitivity, there was a deep current of romanticism in Freud—a sense of the role of impulse, of the drama of life, of the power of symbolism, of ways of knowing that were more poetic than rational in spirit, of the poet's cultural alienation. It was perhaps this romantic sense of drama that led to his gullibility about parental seduction alleged by his first female patients and to his generous susceptibility to the fallacy of the dramatic instance.

Freud also embodies two traditions almost as antithetical as romanticism and nineteenth-century scientism. He was profoundly a Jew, not in a doctrinal sense but in his conception of morality, in his love of the skeptical play of reason, in his distrust of illusion, in the form of his prophetic talent, even in his conception of mature eroticism. His prophetic talent was antithetical to a utopianism either of innocence or of social control. Nor did it lead to a counsel of renunciation. Free oneself of illusion, of neurotic infantilism, and "the soft voice of intellect" would prevail. Wisdom for Freud was neither doctrine nor formula but the achievement of maturity. The patient who is cured is the one who is free enough of neurosis to decide intelligently about his own destiny. As for his conception of mature love, it has always seemed to me that its blend of tenderness and sensuality combined the uxorious imagery of the Hasidic tradition and the sensual quality of the Song of Songs. And might it not have been Freud rather than a commentator of the Haftorahs who said, "In children, it was taught, God gives humanity a chance to make good its mistakes"? The modern trend of permissiveness toward children is surely a feature of the Freudian legacy.

But for all his Hebraic quality, Freud is also in the classical tradition—combining the Stoics and the great Greek dramatists. For Freud as for the Stoics, there is no possibility of man's disobeying the laws of nature. And yet for him it is in this lawfulness that the human drama inheres. His love for Greek drama and his use of it in his formulations are patent. The sense of the human tragedy, the inevitable working out of the human plight—these are the hallmarks of Freud's case histories. When Freud, the tragic dramatist, becomes a therapist, it is not to intervene as a directive authority. The therapist enters the drama of the patient's life, makes possible a play within a play, the transference, and when the patient has "worked through" and understood the drama, he has achieved the wisdom necessary for freedom. Again, like the Stoics, it is in the recognition of one's own nature and in the acceptance of the laws that govern it that the good life is to be found.

Freud's contribution lies in the continuities of which he made us aware. The first of these is the continuity of organic lawfulness. Accident in human affairs was no more to be brooked as "explanation" than was accident in nature. The basis for accepting such an obvious proposition had, of course, been well prepared by a burgeoning nineteenth-century scientific naturalism. It remained for Freud to extend naturalistic explanation to the heart of human affairs. The *Psychopathology of Everyday Life* is not one of Freud's deeper works, but "the

Freudian slip" has contributed more to the common acceptance
of lawfulness in human behavior than perhaps any of the
more rigorous and academic formulations from Wundt to the
present. The forgotten lunch engagement, the slip of the
tongue, the barked shin could no longer be dismissed as accident. Why Freud should have succeeded where novelists,
philosophers, and academic psychologists had failed we shall
consider in a moment.

Freud's extension of Darwinian doctrine beyond Haeckel's
theorem that ontogeny recapitulates phylogeny is another contribution to continuity. It is the conception that, in the human
mind, the primitive, the infantile, and the archaic exist side
by side with the civilized and the evolved:

> Where animals are concerned we hold the view that the most highly
> developed have arisen from the lowest. . . . In the realm of mind,
> on the other hand, the primitive type is so commonly preserved
> alongside the transformations which have developed out of it that
> it is superfluous to give instances in proof of it. When this happens,
> it is usually the result of a bifurcation in development. One quanti-
> tative part of an attitude or an impulse has survived unchanged
> while another has undergone further development. This brings us
> very close to the more general problem of conservation in the
> mind. . . . Since the time when we recognized the error of sup-
> posing that ordinary forgetting signified destruction or annihilation
> of the memory-trace, we have been inclined to the opposite view
> that nothing once formed in the mind could ever perish, that every-
> thing survives in some way or other, and is capable under certain
> conditions of being brought to light again.[1]

What has now come to be common sense is that there is the
potentiality for criminality in every man, and that these are
neither accidents nor visitations of degeneracy, but products of
a delicate balance of forces that under different circumstances
might have produced normality or even saintliness. Good and
evil, in short, grow from a common root.

Freud's genius was in his resolution of polarities. The distinction of child and adult was one. It did not suffice to

[1] *Civilization and Its Discontents* (London: Hogarth Press, 1930),
pp. 14–15.

reiterate that the child was father to the man. The theories of infantile sexuality and the stages of psychosexual development were an effort to fill the gap, the latter clumsy, the former elegant. Though the alleged progression of sexual expression from oral, to anal, to phallic, to genital has not found a secure place either in common sense or in general psychology, the developmental continuity of sexuality has been recognized by both. Common sense honors the continuity in the baby-books and in the permissiveness with which young parents of today resolve their doubts. And the research of Beach and others has shown the profound effects of infantile experience on adult sexual behavior—even in lower organisms.

If today people are reluctant to report their dreams with the innocence once attached to such recitals, it is again because Freud brought into common question the discontinuity between the rational purposefulness of waking life and the seemingly irrational purposelessness of fantasy and dream. While the crude symbolism of Freud's early efforts at dream interpretation has come increasingly to be abandoned, the conception of the dream as representing disguised wishes and fears has become common coin. And Freud's recognition of deep unconscious processes in the creative act has gone far toward enriching our understanding of the kinship between the artist, the humanist, and the man of science.

It is our heritage from Freud that the all-or-none distinction between mental illness and mental health has been replaced by a more humane conception of the continuity of these states. The view that neurosis is a severe reaction to human trouble is as revolutionary in its implications for social practice as it is daring in formulation. The "bad seed" theories, the nosologies of the nineteenth century, the demonologies and doctrines of divine punishment—none of these provided a basis for compassion toward human suffering like that of our time.

One may argue, finally, that Freud's sense of the continuity of human conditions, of the universality of the human predicament, has made possible a deeper sense of the brotherhood of man. It has in any case tempered the spirit of punitiveness toward what once we took as evil and what we now see as sick. We have not yet resolved the dilemma posed by these two ways of viewing: its resolution is one of the great moral challenges of our age.

Why, after such initial resistance, were Freud's views so phenomenally successful in transforming common conceptions of man?

One reason we have already considered: the readiness of the Western world to accept a naturalistic explanation of organic phenomena and, concurrently, to be more prepared for such an explanation in the mental sphere. There had been at least four centuries of uninterrupted scientific progress, finally capped by a theory of evolution that brought man into continuity with the rest of the animal kingdom. The rise of naturalism was a way of understanding nature, and man saw a corresponding decline in the explanatory aspirations of religion. By the close of the nineteenth century, religion, to quote Morton White, "too often agreed to accept the role of a nonscientific spiritual grab-bag, or an ideological know-nothing." Elucidation of the human condition had been abandoned by religion and not yet adopted by science.

It was the inspired imagery, the prototheory of Freud, that was to fill the gap. Success in transforming the common conception of man did not come simply from adopting the cause-and-effect discourse of science. Rather it is Freud's imagery, I think, that provides the clue to his ideological power. It is an imagery of necessity, an imagery that combines the dramatic, the tragic, and the scientific views of necessity. It is here that Freud's is a theory or a prototheory peopled with actors. The characters are from life: the blind, energetic, pleasure-seeking id; the priggish and punitive superego; the ego, battling for its being by diverting the energy of the others to its own use. The drama has economy and terseness. The ego develops canny mechanisms for dealing with the threat of id impulses: denial, projection, and the rest. Balances are struck among the actors, and in this balance are character and neurosis. Freud was using the dramatic technique of decomposition, where the actors are parts of a single life—a technique that he himself had recognized in fantasies and dreams, one which is honored in his essay, "The Poet and the Daydream," and which we have had occasion to discuss earlier.

The imagery of the theory, moreover, has an immediate resonance with the dialectic of experience. True, it is not the stuff of superficial conscious experience. But it fits the human dilemma, its conflict, its private torment, its impulsiveness, its secret and frightening urges, its tragic quality.

In its scientific imagery, the theory is marked by the necessity of the classical mechanics. At times the imagery is hydraulic: suppress one stream of impulses and it breaks out in a displacement elsewhere. The system is closed and mechanical, at times electrical, as when cathexes are formed and withdrawn like electrical charges. Such a way of thought accorded well with the common-sense physics of its age.

Finally, the image of man presented was thoroughly secular; its ideal type was the mature man free of infantile neuroticism, capable of finding his own way. This freedom from both utopianism and asceticism has earned Freud the contempt of ideological totalitarians of the right and the left. But the image has found a ready home in the rising liberal intellectual middle class. For them, the Freudian ideal type has become a rallying point in the struggle against spiritual regimentation.

I have said almost nothing about Freud's equation of sexuality and impulse. That equation surely was and still is a stimulus to resistance. But to say that Freud's success lay in forcing a reluctant Victorian world to accept the importance of sexuality is as empty as it is to hail Darwin for his victory over fundamentalism. Each had a far more profound effect.

Can Freud's contribution to the common understanding of man in the twentieth century be likened to the impact of such great physical and biological theories as Newtonian physics and Darwinian evolution? The question is an empty one. Freud's mode of thought is not a theory in the conventional sense; it is a metaphor, an analogy, a way of conceiving man, a drama. I would propose that Anaximander is the proper parallel: his view of the connectedness of physical nature was also an analogy, and a powerful one. Freud's work is the ground from which theory will grow, and he has prepared the twentieth century to nurture the growth. But, far more important, he has provided an image of man that has made him comprehensible without at the same time making him contemptible.

Fate and the Possible

Through history, man's notions about fate have corresponded to his changing ideas about himself. By setting forth some propositions about man's present conception of himself and his world and examining them closely, we may perhaps be able to draw some conclusions about the role of fate in an age of science.

1. A first proposition might be put this way. Man does not deal directly with nature; nature is a symbolic construct, a creature of man's powers to represent experience through powerful abstractions. As Ernst Cassirer might put it, man lives in a symbolic world of his own collective creation, a symbolic world that has as one of its principal functions the ordering and explication of experience. A change in one's conception of the world involves not simply a change in what one encounters but also in how one translates it.

2. Man's image of himself, perforce, is not independent of his image of the world. *Weltanschauung* places limits on and gives shape to *Selbstanschauung*. For it is characteristic of man not only that he creates a symbolic world but also that he then becomes its servant by conceiving of his own powers as limited by the powers he sees outside himself.

3. Perhaps the chief vehicle in the relation between man's subjective sense of himself and his sense of the world of nature is the idea of fate. Fate is that which is beyond one's control; it is an outer limit.

4. The inverse of fate is the sense of potency—what we

think is possible for us. That is to say, our view of fate shapes our sense of potency, and vice versa. Fate is the residuum that is left after one has run through the census of what is humanly possible. Each discovery of a way of proceeding, of a way of discovering, forestalling, or effecting, is, then, an incursion into fate that in effect rolls back what we take fate to be. There may one day be a beautiful formula that goes something like this: $e = p/f$, where e is the sense of human effectiveness, p the value of all outcomes thought to be determined by human effort, and f the value of all outcomes thought to be determined by fate.

5. The degree to which a society elaborates a technology determines the amount of division of labor in the society. The rationale of a technology is that its tools are not such that each individual can be equipped with a full set of them. With technological advance more things are possible, but social and technical organization is increasingly necessary to bring them off. In effect, then, the sense of potency—the idea of the possible—increases in scope, but the artificer of the possible is now society rather than the individual.

6. And one final proposition. Man's working image of himself is anchored in his sense of intimacy—in the events and relations that are the fabric of his immediate experience and make up his way of life. Change in the individual is a function of how much and in what manner an intimate way of life is altered.

Before exploring the consequences of these premises, there should be a word about the psychological structure of fate. At one extreme we may speak of a peopled fate, a realm over which one has no control, where purposeful and personalized forces operate. Dodds has given us a searching examination of the peopled fate of the classic Greeks in his *The Greeks and the Irrational*. At the other extreme is the view of fate as embodied in mathematical statistics and statistical mechanics. Fate is here equated with a conception of residual variance—the set of all remaining causes that cannot be accounted for because of ignorance or, if all were known, pure unknowable randomness. The secular view of fate pits man as a systematic and controlling intelligence against ignorance and chaos. The religious view of fate pits man against a pantheon of controlling spirits.

In tracing the impact of science on man's image of himself, we might remind ourselves of the series of psychological upsets that served, presumably, to diminish that image. The fall of the heliocentric universe pushed man from the center of things, relegating him to a position on one of the satellites orbiting around a not very major star. The emergence of understanding about electricity and magnetism made it clear that one could no longer conceive of energy solely in the analogy of the human arm. The doctrine of evolution is said to have robbed man of his image of himself as unique. And within our own generation, Freud's insights have questioned man's rationalistic vanity in a degree comparable to the onslaught that nuclear fission and fusion have made on man's remaining sense of safety against annihilation by forces that are uncontrollable once freed.

Yet, if we look at the last century and man's changing image of himself, obviously we do not find man cringing before a swollen, chaotic fate. The style of the West, the style of the newly emerging states—with Nigeria's scheduling of the opening of five schools a month over a ten-year period—and even the style of the two most powerful Communist states are premised upon widely expanded conceptions of the possible: the technologically possible and the humanly possible. When one looks more deeply, there are new strains, to be sure, new forms of helplessness, new ways of defining incapacity. A modern Job might come to terms with the death of a child as science's failure to prevent this particular disease or death. But new also is the form of grief that leads one to give to a research institution so that others may be saved from dying senselessly.

There appear to be three loci of change that should be considered in discussing our propositions. The first is in the transition that occurs as man alters his image of fate and pre-empts the powers that were before seen as fateful. A second lies in the process of depersonalizing fate. Finally, there is change in the recognition that a scientific technology involves increasing dependence upon specialism within the society.

Perhaps the deepest but quietest change over the last century has been in man's view of himself as an intelligence. To put it more accurately, the change is less in his view of himself than in his conception of men as knowers, of their collective product, science. The idea of discovery as a result of engineered tinkering has given way to the concept of science as an enterprise of thinking—imperfectly understood, to be sure, but intuitively appreciated. The archetype of Edison as ingenious inventor has been replaced by one of Einstein as powerful thinker. The philosophical crises of our university seminars—Gödel's theorem of the inevitable paradox that is generated by any self-contained system of propositions, the principle of complementarity wherein certain forms of knowledge canonically exclude others, and the logico-linguistic relativities of Wittgenstein's "word games"—are finding their way into common sense and understanding as surely as did Newton's conceptions.

What has emerged as a result of this ferment is a reflective concern with the nature of knowledge and with the forms of intelligence that make knowledge possible. Indeed, out of our philosophical and scientific understanding of the informational processes we have created a new technology for the use of artificial intelligence as executed by computer programs. Not only have we reduced random fatefulness in industrial technology; we have delegated the policing of it to machine processes conceived of not as an extension of our arm but as an extension of our intelligence.

The depersonalization of fate is so deeply part of the history of the Western trend toward secularism that it cannot be treated apart from it. It is in the collapse of transcendental doctrines that we see the effects most clearly. In the first instance, there was the discomfort and disruption that came with the passing of religious absolutes, with the weakening of canons of absolute truth and goodness. Since then, it is interesting that we have either sought new guidance in the form of ersatz secular absolutes or have moved toward an intrinsic definition of the good and the beautiful from "inside out." There has been the secular absolutism of the right, with its deification of the state and racial destiny and with its genocide. On the equally absolute left, there has been the sanctification of a Marxist-Hegelian doctrine of historical inevitability, an inevitability that needed the support of police methods. Both solutions have been violently anti-intellectual, opposed to the definition of ideals in terms of individual reason and individual compassion. In the center, the effort has been to find a conception of rightness in an examination of the nature of man, to seek a humane ethic based not on an economic or political or religious view of man but on a psychological one.

There is perhaps no more meaningful index of this change than the manner in which we view children and their education. In one century we have moved from the moralism of McGuffey and his *Readers* to, and perhaps beyond, the child-centered and sometimes mawkish compassion of Dewey. It is Freud who gives the text: effectiveness is not a product of utopia but rests upon insight into the human condition. Indeed, the reform movement we see in American education today, the cultivation of individual excellence as an ideal, again moves from the inside out. It is an attempt to roll back fate through the increase of intellectual potency.

Finally, there is the revolution in society and economy that sprang from a century of technological and scientific innovation. The century has seethed with innovations in imagery, efforts to find a new balance between a conception of society and a conception of man. We have witnessed new patterns of socialist organization and ideology in which social welfare has been converted from a political slogan into a difficult and not altogether consistent principle of administrative planning. Capitalism has altered its stance from the romanticism of perfect economic competition to a doctrine of public-service oligopoly. It would be difficult to infer from the British White Paper of 1925 on colonial education what in fact happened after the Second World War in Britain's wisely subtle liquidation of her overseas empire.

We are groping toward an arrangement of our industrial society, and the advent of automation makes the outcome unclear. The steady American trend over the past half century has been toward a universal middle class, with increasingly equal access to consumer goods made possible by steadily rising incomes falling within an ever narrower range. The prevailing ideal in this middle-class enterprise is "good management," a modestly activist image based again on confidence in the application of trained intelligence. We are as much shocked at Belgium's poor management of the transition in the Congo as we are by her earlier attitude of exploitation. It is perhaps most characteristic of our national enterprise that the concept of management rather than a doctrine of "planning" has become central. Management is planning that is subject to moment-by-moment revision by human intelligence. While it, like most emerging conceptions, is vaguely defined, its core is the exercise of decision based on human appraisal. That theories of decision making abound today is no historical accident.

Finally, what is the impact of all we have considered on the intimacy of life? Our ways have been changed not only by technology but by the new images of living that technology has made possible. Yet our taming of fate and our skills in the management of enterprises has created malaise. We hear much of the search for identity. There has developed a wide disparity between our sense of what is possible and the private ways in which we live our immediate lives. The impact of the century has been powerfully and irreversibly energizing—but the sense of effectiveness, that resultant term in my mock formula for the relation of potency and fate, has not been given its full chance for expression. What we have now is a new frontier, a frontier for the full use of human beings. Perhaps I reveal my biases as a psychologist when I say that the cultivation of this frontier excites me far more than the prospects of exploring empty space.

Speaking at Massachusetts Institute of Technology in 1960, Edwin Land remarked that we had been puny in our conception of the new professions that are possible for men. Given, for example, the vast underdeveloped areas of the world, how do we arrange the use of our own human resources to bring these areas into the modern age speedily and without untoward suffering? Or, given the vast increase in knowledge in all fields of learning, how do we equip our men and women to impart that knowledge to new generations? I am not speaking of moral equivalents of war in James's sense: that is much too modest a conception. Rather, it is in developing the arts of peace that we shall find an expression for the new images that the century has produced. Until then, we shall not become the full beneficiaries of the change that science has wrought. A people who feel that they are living at the full limit of what is possible will have no crises of identity. Our challenge now is to use those portions of fate that we have taken over.

Psychology and the Image of Man

One sometimes agrees to deliver a lecture on a set theme, only to discover that the theme is not quite what one had expected. Having agreed to deliver a Herbert Spencer Lecture in Oxford on how psychology had affected common sense about man or had itself been affected by that common sense—thinking then that it would make an amusing summer interlude of historical writing—I soon discovered it would not go so easily. For once I had started on the inevitable first notes, it was plain to me that I was not embarked at all on a summer of intellectual history but on a much thornier enterprise, partly philosophical, partly psychological, and only trivially historical—trivial in the sense that it was no surprise that, in the later nineteenth century, psychology had modelled itself on those successful natural science neighbors in whose district it had decided to build its mansion, and had suffered the consequences thereafter.

I can recall my early dark thoughts. Little question, to begin with, that the most powerful impact on common sense had come from Freud. Yet Freud was, and is, peripheral to and grossly atypical of academic psychology, so much so, indeed, that apart from providing cautionary methodological tales with which to warn the unwary undergraduate, his work is not even covered in the Oxford syllabus. Or take it another way: has psychology affected issues of public concern on which it could reasonably be expected to have a bearing, say economics? Here, surely, is a powerful mode of thought and of policy-making that treats psychological matters like risk, preference, delayed gratification in saving and investment. It even proposes notions like utility through which the values and probabilities of outcomes are assumed to combine to determine choice. Yet though economics had, in the lifetime of official psychology, been through the revolutions of Marshall, of Keynes, of Schumpeter, and of Morgenstern and van Neumann, there is not a trace of any influence exerted by psychologists. A minor exception, perhaps, is in the application of psychology to industrial relations—a not altogether successful venture at that, and one also sufficiently peripheral to psychology to be ignored (perhaps deservedly) in the syllabus of most major university departments.

And finally, since I do not wish to make too much of my initial gloomy thoughts, let me remark on the strange fact that, in recent years, the most conspicuous public voice of psychology has been radically Utopian and reductionist, motivated by the assertion that scientific psychology shows that the human enterprise is altogether wrongly conceived, that it would be better managed by human engineers than by law and that when ordinary people acted human they were muddled by notions like choice, freedom, dignity, intention, expectations, goals, and the like. B. F. Skinner, in his Herbert Spencer Lecture two years ago, implied indeed that human affairs so conceived could be shown to be "wrong" in much the same way as Copernicus had shown that the heliocentric universe was "wrong."

My winter of discontent did indeed lead me to explore the impact of psychology on common sense—and vice versa—but it lead me also to look more deeply into what might be called the interface between "expert psychology" on the one side and the common-sense views of man on the other. I was drawn to a disturbing conclusion on the matter of why experimental or academic psychology had not had more of an impact on the broad cultural conception of the nature of man or why, perhaps, its contribution had been negatively reductionist. It was not that psychology had not yet found out enough, was not empirically advanced enough to enter the debate with authority. Rather it was the stronger conclusion that psychology had initially defined its task in such a way that it could never have had much of a direct impact, given the nature of its concepts of explanation. Its initial concerns, its theoretical orientation, its style of research were not fitted to the kinds of processes or patterns that shape human affairs as they occur in human societies: symbolic systems like language, conceptual structures in terms of which human beings carve up and interpret the world around them, and the cultural constraints imposed by human institutions were not within its terms of reference. These systems include everyday concepts like purpose, mind, responsibility, loyalty, even Cabinet responsibility—transmitted concepts that serve as the basis for human institutions like the law and economic exchange, institutions which, so to speak, provide a buffer against individual variation.

The founding contract of academic psychology was such that, in the main, these matters were ruled out as belonging elsewhere, or, more accurately, as nothing but second-order phenomena to be derived from first principles. The larger edifice of human affairs, it was felt, would be elucidated by the stones that comprised it. We had, I believe, painted ourselves into a very tight little corner where we had much control and certainty—like lower computer specialists who insist that their task is to describe the hardware and the machine language and not the properties of the programs they comprise—and the price we may have had to pay had we followed on this way would have been perpetual and justifiable modesty.

There are historical reasons why this was so, stemming from our early childhood of envy among the natural sciences and our attempts to emulate (or, better, simulate) their successes, and I shall consider these in a moment. It seems to me that I have not exaggerated. Indeed, I am sure that there are still psychologists of the highest intelligence and good will who would insist today that the course upon which we originally embarked is a sound one for psychology, but after forty years of participating in the enterprise with mounting contrary conviction, I would be less than candid if I did not call it as I saw it. Indeed, I am encouraged to air my conclusions because I think that winds of change are blowing and that one can already sense the new course on which we are embarking.

All of this is *not* to say, please note, that psychology has not got on with it. For it certainly has. But our modest successes have all been, in a special way, *in vitro,* treating chunks of behavior out of the controlling contexts in which they ordinarily occur, even though the contexts have a massive influence over the chunks. The more rigorously isolated from context and the more tightly controlled the conditions of experiment, the more precise and the more modest the results have been. The justification of course has been that this is the traditional way to proceed in a line of inquiry called "the natural sciences," refining one's investigative procedure to a paradigm or model that is presumed to elucidate phenomena in real life. This brave and bold approach doubtless worked in physics, where the connection between controlled experiment and nature had become clear. For reasons that will concern us in a moment, it is not plain that such a program is yet suitable to psychology or will ever be. The disturbing symptom in our discipline has been its steady loss of conceptual unity. It increasingly consists of a collection of topics-cum-procedures, between which it is ever more difficult to discern workable conceptual connections. Each topic develops its paradigm and its literature, even its own heroes. Recently, Alan Allport (1975) has expressed the concern that each topic has a way of digging itself into an isolated trench, with less and less connection even with the neighboring trenches, the end of the digging being reached not through success but boredom. Again, let me insist that this is not to say that some of the topics have not been of the greatest interest—the study of human perception being a conspicuous case of one topical success after another. But perception, on the other hand, is studied *in vitro,* and efforts to relate perception to motivation or to learning or to social behavior each begin as a new topic-cum-procedure.

Let me move on to a more detailed diagnosis of our historical difficulties, better to come to terms with what I think is needed to rescue psychology from its past and perhaps to assure it a place in the general debate on the nature of man.

Psychology paid its price of admission to the natural sciences in the nineteenth century by a tacit agreement to ban both mind and purpose from its past armamentarium of explanatory concepts. A decent nineteenth-century natural science had no truck with either mentalism or teleology. And, indeed, given the ghost-in-the-machine use of such concepts in that period, neither of them deserved a place. To anybody conversant with the history of psychology over the past century, it is surely plain that such an initial taboo could not be sustained, save in the form of an ideological preface. Mentalistic concepts were there all along—in Titchener's method of structural introspection, in concepts like 'imagery,'' and even in the hallowed doctrine of threshold and just-noticeable-difference. And intentionality was surely an implicit premise in theories of attention, with notions like "set" being used heuristically to deal with self-directed intentions to behave in a certain way. Indeed, we preferred to conceive of these as mental-like phenomena or purposive-like behaviors, as in Tolman's purposive behaviorism. Even the period of radical behaviorism, ushered in by J. B. Watson and now perhaps flickering to a close in the polemics of Professor Skinner, was, we should remember, accompanied by a rise of the phenomenological theories of Gestalt psychologists who, you will recall, insisted upon a distinction between man's physical or geographical environment and the effective phenomenal or behavioral environment that mediated between a world of physics and the world of experience as it affected man's conduct.

Three concerns of post-war psychology further hastened the trend away from radical behaviorism: the emergence of so-called "cognitive psychology," with massive reliance on concepts like hypothesis, strategies, expectations. Cognitive psychology soon found common cause with artificial intelligence, whose heuristic spirit was not in the least constrained by a fixation on the nineteenth century. The third hastening trend has been the arousal of interest among psychologists in the nature and use of language and other man-made rule systems.

In spite of all this, much of psychology has remained true (perhaps because there is something compelling about infantile fixation) to its early vow. We are still embarrassed by the possibility that purpose and intention will suck us back into the swamp of teleology. Mentalism and teleology are still four-letter words in psychology. And here is where the difficulty arises, I think, but in a rather surprising way.

For while we have become increasingly free of our ancient phobias about mind and purpose—most of us now being willing to treat them at least in the "as if" spirit of a heuristic—we have not altogether freed ourselves of the positivistic bias that goes with the older style of "hard-nosed" research. Let me explain more fully what I mean by this. The contrast that is relevant, I think, is between what can be called a structural approach and a point-by-point sequential approach.

Let me use as a typical example the notion of a stimulus and a response, the two of them being defined independently of each other. A light comes on or a buzzer sounds and an organism responds to it, the response again being an it. Stimuli and responses are then, in some sense, said to be connected or related, or the occurrence of a response after the appearance of a stimulus is said to change in probability by virtue of some condition either in the stimulus presentation beforehand or in the consequences that follow the pairing, what is often called a reinforcement. Stimuli and responses have a kind of thing or event status, and each can be operationally defined—the former as a nonsense syllable or a light flash or what not; the latter, the response, of course, being an observable event like a button press or a verbal response.

Perhaps the first sign that all was not well in this positivistic heaven came as an offshoot of the theory of information, when it was shown that the nature of a stimulus could not be defined merely in centimetres, grams, and seconds, but also depended upon the ensemble of alternative stimuli that might have occurred, how many bits of information were transmitted, or more succinctly, what was the uncertainty in the event. Well, that could also be dealt with by a sleight of hand in which the set of permissible stimuli to be presented was controlled by the experimenter, and probability of occurrence could then be stated as another property of the stimulus—so that to c, g, and s could be added p. But suppose, now, the set of alternatives were not independent of each other but, rather, were part of a structure, a structure whose existence was in the head or mind of the subject, like his language and its rules. How are we to interpret the comprehension of a sentence?

Take an example from the linguist C. V. Fillmore (1971): May we come in? Is it a stimulus? Well, not really. The sentence itself appears, rather, to be a complex function which seems to be mapping a context into a proposition that "carries" a certain meaning. The elements are more like triggers than stimuli. "May" signals a speech act requesting permission and recognizes that the addressee(s) is on his own turf as defined by some code. "We" signals that one should consider contexts involving at least three participants in which at least one is the addressee, etc. "Come" indicates that the speaker and his companions want to move towards the addressee or to where he will be when they all get there, and contrasts with "go"; it involves spatial deixis. "In" signals that the destination is enclosed, container-like—a room, a house, a pub, a sauna.

In order to translate such a sentence into a proposition one would need to know not only how the addresser and addressee organize their worlds, but also to have some hypotheses about where they might be or even what they are doing. The sentence might have been uttered by a dentist on behalf of himself and his nurse, the two poised with drill, addressing a patient open-mouthed on the chair! One could make no sense of such a sentence without taking into account the cognitive structures in terms of which the world is organized by the participants and, indeed, how language maps into those structures. The notion of a self-contained stimulus (or response) fades as, indeed, does a simple sequential account of the order of processing between input and final output. And what is the output?

Most of what humans respond to in the so-called real world has this property: without a structural description of the cognitive organization in the minds of the participants in an action, one cannot even locate, still less define the stimulus. Indeed, we have long been warned about this difficulty, even before our linguistic colleagues forced us to confront it. Was it not Sir Frederic Bartlett who argued so persuasively the impossibility of a theory of memory based on the storage and retrieval of such isolated elements as nonsense syllables? I think I have made clear enough what I intend by structure for us to go on to the next point.

It is another heritage of psychology's early alliance with nineteenth-century natural sciences that it cut itself off from considering the possibility that mental structures derive from what anthropologists call "culture": a society's set of theories, values, ways of acting, and thinking and respecting. Hoping to keep its biological base, to remain with the *Naturwissenschaften* rather than suffer the denigration of being a *Geisteswissenschaft,* psychology chose to avoid questions of how human beings were able to operate with such complex rule systems as kinship, economic exchange, and the law, and did so in a most extraordinary way. It could keep its attention focused inside the individual skin (rather than upon the culture) by invoking a response system: call it a tendency to conform to social norms. Men had a tendency to conform, and in conformity-demanding situations normal distributions of response were transformed into J-curves. At least, two differentiable types of situations were thereby recognized, although the statistical criterion thus provided was not really used very searchingly. But then, it is not a very searching analysis of the rules of chess, or courtship, or investment, to say simply that people conform to them. As Roger Barker (1963) has been fond of pointing out, the best predicator of human behavior is a specification of where the person is: in post-offices, we *do* behave post-office.

The effects of these three historical habits that have so dogged psychology—its anti-mentalism, its tendency towards positivism of the old school, and its refusal to consider in detail how a culture patterns human action—put psychology in a curious light. It has come, in some inevitable way, to stand as a champion of reductionism, often against its will and its spirit. Partly this is because the three historical deformations are reductionist in their very nature: if you think responses are all and mind is a nonsense, if you do not take into account the structural complexity of what it is that men respond to, and if you take man to be a creature of biology tempered by a certain amount of learning, then it is a very dim picture indeed that one offers in the debate about man's nature.

But there is also something in the nature of the research we do as a result of our positivist tradition which tempts the reader of our results into reductionism. It stems from our built-in fascination with the methodology of one or at most three independent variables at a time and our delight in finding experimental situations where such small numbers of variables do account for a large part of the variance. I would offer as an example in my own field of developmental studies the extremely catastrophic experimental situations used by Harlow and his associates to demonstrate the enormous importance of terry-cloth clinging in the young rhesus monkey's attachment to a mother surrogate. Doubtless, when all else fails, terry cloth will do. But compare Harlow's results with the subtleties that have emerged from studying infant mother interactions *in situ* reported this year by the ethologist Robert Hinde in his Wolfson Lecture.

You might think that having said all that, I would now don sackcloth and ashes, resign my Watts Professorship in the University of Oxford and slink away to do penance, or perhaps battle. Not in the slightest! As I have already hinted, all is not lost. Consider my Oxford microcosm. Professor Weiskrantz is busily at work studying how certain brain lesions produce a state of "blind-sight" as he calls it, in which his patients manage to be able to supply correct answers to questions about visual events they have been presented with of which they claim to have no direct awareness. He would not blench if you congratulated him on his interesting work on the neurology of consciousness. My own work is shot through with reference to the role of intention in early language acquisition—intention as exhibited by the child and as perceived by the mother. And my distinguished colleague Dr. Broadbent is studying business games the better to understand how businessmen, civil servants, and politicians come to policy decisions. He would not stoop, I assure you, to the low-level nonsense of the leader-writer on *The Times* who found nothing more enlightening to say about the government's efforts to get hold of the sterling exchange crisis than that it was acting like Pavlov's dog now hitting the lending rate button, now the import control level, and so on.

The three of us, I suspect, are straws in the wind, and I would like to say why I think so by examining briefly how psychology is coping with mind and intention, how we are faring in efforts to get hold of the structural contexts that determine the underlying significance of "stimuli," so-called, and how finally I see hope for psychology joining forces with the sciences of culture, even perhaps including economics. Having done that, I would like to pay a tribute to Freud, an appreciation of why he caught and transformed our thinking about man. Perhaps we can then assess what it takes to affect common sense.

Mind, intention, and culture. Let me look first at "mind" and "purpose" to see how these might be faring—whether psychology is addressing anything to common sense aside from spirited tracts about the non-existence of both of these in the style of the village atheist. To locate ourselves we shall need some analysis first.

I shall begin with the common sense distinction between "intended" or purposeful behavior in contrast to "caused" behavior. We say of intended action that it is carried out "for the sake of" achieving an end in mind, in contrast to caused behavior which is understood to be contingently related to a set of antecedent conditions. Typically, the cause of a behavior is determined by a method in which we control a set of antecedent conditions defined independently of the consequent behavior that the antecedents may be found to produce. When a relation is found between the antecedent and consequent, we invoke a contingent link between the two, usually in the form of a "mechanism" or "hypothetical construct." That, in any case, is the surface structure of what we do. In fact, there is much that is implicit in our selection of both the antecedent conditions, the consequent behavior, and the intervening contingent construct. For example, if it should be the case, as it most certainly would be, that the incidence of diarrhea in infants is highly correlated with the antecedent softness of asphalt highways, we would immediately recognize that this is an "empty correlation" and we would look for a more sensible link between antecedent and consequent, like the temperature limits for the culturing of a relevant baccilus. "Theories" are what provide the causal glue between antecedents and consequents, but only certain kinds of theories.

Where the analysis of intended action is concerned, the principal objection is, of course, that to invoke intention as explanation is circular, that it explains nothing. Such explanations cannot help in the search for antecedents. But is the use of intention limited in this way? Antecedents and consequents must obviously be defined independently lest one become involved in the dizzy enterprise against which Hume warned us of defining the antecedent by the consequent, and vice versa. "Why did he attend Congregation?" "Because he wanted to." "Because he did." Plainly, explanation of the antecedent why of behavior gets nowhere by this route.

But now, let me pose two questions about explanation by cause and description by intention. The first is a question of distinguishability, the second of consequentialness. I shall be crude, I am not a philosopher. But psychologists trying to get their house in order must use philosophical analysis, and therefore, you will hear overtones (probably out of tune) of G. E. M. Anscombe, Quine, John Searle, Charles Taylor, and Rom Harre. If Wittgenstein was right, that the philosopher's task is to help the fly out of the bottle, I can only hope there will be a Wittgenstein in the wings.

I begin with the well-known example of two utterances that are both distinguishable and differ widely in their consequences: one is "I am going to take a walk," and the other, "I am going to be sick." The first implies that something is under my control as an agent. The latter implies a prediction made on the basis of antecedent sensations, and agency is not implied. In the first utterance, a noncontingent link is implied between intention and action. If a contingent link were intended, I would have said something like "The chances are I am going to take a walk," which would be an appropriate reply to the question, "What do you think you will be doing next Sunday morning?" Now, the category distinction between actions implying intention and behaviors that do not is made all the time in all languages, all cultures, and is irresistible. I am ignoring for the moment whether, in Professor Skinner's curious sense, it is pre-copernican or "wrong" as a description, for that at present is irrelevant. The distinction is made and it is a compelling feature of man's experience.

As Mrs. Anscombe is at pains to point out, the consequences of the distinction are serious. Failure to do what one said one would do is, in the case of intentional actions, interpretable as lying (though extenuating circumstances are recognized). Failure in the second case is interpretable only as a mistake, unless one reinterprets the statement to be an intentional effort to deceive, but then it is relocated in the first category. At this point, very different consequences in terms of the behavior of others toward the speaker can be expected. Different Gricean cooperative principles apply. Mistakes are expected: lies are not. The first produce disappointment, the second indignation.

Now we may note that both lying and mistake-making are also amenable to analysis by antecedents: the liar may be more likely to be the child of a broken home: the mistake-maker may have undergone permissive schooling, but that is not the issue. The issue, rather, is whether the act in question was experienced as a lie or a mistake, whether something is or is not intentional. If the latter, if an intention is carried out, no further questioning need be asked.

For it is taken as axiomatic by human beings that what we do is congruent with what we intend to do. Only the exceptions require analysis. When intention is not carried out, contingency is not permitted as extenuating. Intention and execution are assumed to be structurally linked. Extenuating circumstances for an unfulfilled intention are either changed intention—"I decided not to go for a walk when I heard that lions were loose in the park," or alien forces—"I was locked into my room." There is no objective test available for determining whether a "real" intention exists in the person who proclaims it. Intentions are inferred or attributed on the basis of conventional contexts and their recognition conditions depend upon what, in contemporary philosophical jargon, is known as "uptake." To describe an intention and the action on behalf of it is to give a structural description of an event as it is interpreted by the participants.

It is much as with a speech act. The intention implied in a speech act does not cause the procedures that are used in its execution, whether syntactic or semantic. But as Searle properly notes, the role of these in the meaning of the sentence cannot be analyzed without attributing an intent to the act: to inform, to warn, to praise, etc. If one says, "Would you be so kind as to pass the salt?" the constituents are to be understood in terms of a request that is made contrastive to a command, and not to be understood in terms of what it appears to be on the surface: a question about the limits of the addressee's compassion. The effort is to define the structure of a set of constituents in an act. And that is what we do when we assign an act to an intention structure.

The argument, thus far, is simply that human beings can and irresistibly do distinguish certain acts of their fellow men as intentional, that we see others as having something in mind and behaving on behalf of what they have in mind. Our response towards them and their acts is sharply affected by whether we categorize it as intentional. The argument extends beyond that. It would be a vain enterprise to explain or even to discuss the causes of any human behavior without taking into account whether or not intention had been attributed. At least where social or transactional behavior is concerned, even the causal chain between antecedent and consequent must contain an account of how the participants categorized each other's acts.

What all this suggests, at the very least, is that we adopt "the perception of intention" and "the perception of mindfulness" as topics for research. We could at least find out what "cues" lead us to "see" certain behaviors as intentional acts or as leading to the inference that somebody or some thing is in possession of a "mind." Let it be said immediately that there is a flourishing "topic" in psychology, inspired by Fritz Heider (1958), that deals with just this issue, called "attribution theory." A recent incisive review by E. E. Jones (1976) suggests that there is indeed pay dirt here. Not surprisingly, people do distinguish between action caused by circumstances and action caused by intent, and with devastating consequences for their evaluation of what they have observed. To illustrate, when they themselves are involved in a situation, they are much more likely to see their own behavior as a result of circumstances. When they observe others, they see the action as produced by intention (when it is conventional or expected) or by quirky dispositional traits steering intention (when the behavior is unconventional or unexpected).

"Actors attribute to situations what observers attribute to actors" appear to be one conclusion. But the general conclusion from this work is that "Behavior belongs to the person: the 'field' acts on everyone." Yet the research has not really found the so-called cues by which the inference of intent is made. For, in fact, there are no simple cues in the conventional sense. What is involved is a structural inference, based on a constellation of events. In this sense, it is precisely as in linguistics. What is the cue by which we recognize a dependent clause or an imbedding? It is not marked by parentheses or tree diagrams, but inferred from the understanding of the rules of a sentence.

Stimulus and the anticipated input. I commented on the fact that the inference of intent was at once ubiquitous, universal, and irresistible. And indeed, one could go on to explore the biological roots of such perceptions. Heider and Simmel long ago produced an animated film involving the movement of squares, triangles, and circles which is compelling seen as animate figures involved in a scenario of intent, much as Michotte has a like film for inanimate causality. There is little question that intention movements in lower organisms trip off appropriate, goal-linked behavior in their conspecifics, and Menzel (1974) has recently shown the manner in which young chimpanzees use the direction of locomotion of a better informed animal to guide their own search for a hidden reward object. Indeed the past two decades of research in neuro-physiology suggest that there is a feed-forward mechanism in neural functioning by which to put it metaphorically, an about-to-occur action is transmitted by an efference copy of that action around the nervous system. As von Holst and Mittelstaedt (1950) put it nearly thirty years ago, input stimuli do not impinge upon a neutral organism, but are processed by a comparator against anticipated input—the monkey knows when his hand is being shaken by a stick and when he is shaking the stick.

The perceptual processing of the organism that yields inferences of intent seems not to be all that illusory as an account of what is going on in the nervous system. Not only is there good reason to believe that human behavior is in fact organized into acts carried out "for the sake" of achieving certain ends, but also the receptive human nervous system is ready to perceive behavior as so structured, perhaps too ready. It should follow, then, that any description on human behavior must take into account this powerful if loose program of perceptual processing if it is to predict how human beings are going to behave in an environment containing other human beings. It must do so in the same spirit as the linguist who takes into account the fact that human beings process strings of words as sentences or the student of perception who takes into account the fact that human perceivers organize input into figure-ground configurations.

But I must reiterate that societies prescribe rules and codes based on the kinds of perceptions and inferences we have been discussing. People starve to death biologically for these codes, turn away from sexual attractions, go to war, etc. All of these domains are more or less tightly regulated by systems of roles, of rules, of exchange, etc. Increasingly, anthropologists are developing formal procedures for describing such rule systems. Increasingly, psychologists are becoming interested in how such rule systems are acquired, and it is certainly not by the conventional linking of stimuli and responses.

The implication of all that I have said is certainly not just that we consider psychological phenomena at different "levels," this one molecular, a next one molar, still another yet more molar, *ad infinitum*. It is more revolutionary than that, I think. The conclusion is that a reaction to any feature of an environment is, to use Chomsky's (1976) phrase, most likely to be "structure dependent." By structure dependency he means, and I mean, that the significance of any feature is determined by its position in a structure. The position of a piece on a chessboard, the function of a word in a sentence, a particular facial expression, the color or placement of a light, these cannot be interpreted without reference to the person's internalized rules of chess or language, the conventions he holds concerning human interaction, the traffic rules in force in his mind. To set out with even so innocently positivistic an objective as studying, say, the threshold for recognizing different colors is a surprisingly empty exercise without a notion of how colors are contextualized in the task. Some years ago, for example, Postman and I showed (1949) that the recognition threshold for the color red varied in exposure time by a full order of magnitude depending upon whether red was conventionally expected in that setting or not.

What then is the status of experiments that strip expectancy down to a level, say, of chromatic equiprobability? It is said that by so doing one obtains a "neutral" situation which permits one to explore the basic "color discrimination" mechanism. What is basic in this context? Well, it turns out to be the case under fairly simple conditions that the recognizability of colors to which one has been previously exposed is a function of their linguistic codability—roughly the number of elements in the linguistic description required to differentiate them from other colors in the array presented. Are not linguistic codability and expectancy as basic to a theory of color perception and color recognition as the spectral composition of the input?

It would seem to me—and this is very much in the spirit of the late Egon Brunswik—that the task of psychology as an experimental discipline is to investigate representative settings in which phenomena are contextualized in order to come anywhere near approximating what might be called a systematic description of ordinary behavior. If it cannot do this, it cannot achieve generality. But far worse than that. It risks ending up peddling paradigms designed more for narrow nicety than for descriptive or explanatory power, as in theories of learning where attentional factors are minimized to a point approaching zero, and where, it would seem, context and materials are designed for achieving maximum experimental control rather than representativeness.

My emphasis on structure sensitivity in "natural" situations leads me to look for leads in linguistics. For I admire linguistics not only for its willingness to look at natural, ordinary behavior —speaking of comprehending ordinary speech—but for its aim of describing the banal and the ordinary systematically. If I ask a linguist about sentences, he will not insist that we confine our discussion to the movements of lips, tongue, and glottis. If I ask him about reading, he will not go on about cross-modal matching. Chomsky, in his recent *Reflections on Language,* has an interesting point to make. He begins with what he chooses to call "science making," the manner in which people ordinarily put knowledge together. In some domains, this human capacity appears to be extraordinarily powerful, as in the creating of physical sciences and mathematics, in other domains rather feeble, as in matters involving people exercising their will.

Science making, whether lay-modest or grand, depends upon a human capacity to make structure-sensitive distinctions and to do so easily, immediately, and with a minimum of prior tuition on the point at issue. There is, as always with Chomsky, an insistence that the capacity involved is innate, by which he means that certain capacities are species specific, including the human capacity to organize knowledge in a human way—with which I find no quarrel. One of these natural capacities is, of course, the faculty to proceed with astonishing speed and facility into the uses of language. He then goes on to say:

Alongside the language faculty and interacting with it in the most intimate way is the faculty of mind that we might call "common sense understanding," a system of beliefs, expectations, and knowledge, concerning the nature and behavior of objects, their place in a system of "natural kinds," the organization of these categories, and the properties that determine the categorization of objects and the analysis of events. A general "innateness hypothesis" will also include principles that bear on the place and role of people in a social world, the nature and conditions of work, the structure of human action, will and choice, and so on. These systems may be unconscious for the most part and even beyond the reach of conscious introspection.

The starting point for Chomsky, then, would be to examine the natural ways, or better, the ecological representative ways, to use Brunswik's term, in which people look at and account for objects involved in events and how they look at and account for people and their actions.

As I read Chomsky, he is proposing that we begin our inquiry into the nature of human functioning with a structural description of ordinary knowing, to set as our goal the elucidation of those structures as we find them. It is the ordinariness of the enterprise that appeals to me. For it is just such ordinariness that has so often been lost from psychology in its efforts to deal positivistically with isolated variables. It is

what has led us in the past to get stuck in little trenches la-
belled "serial position curve" when the intent was to study
memory. This is changing. It is not that we had to build upon
the dreary, pioneering studies of Ebbinghaus on the rote
learning of nonsense syllables, but to escape, to run away from
our adoptive home. The study of memory like much else in
psychology is beginning again to concern itself with what people ordinarily do when they remember, even with what they
do to save themselves from having to remember. The study of
cognition in general, with its new emphasis on natural categories, is making striking progress. Developmental psychology,
as it moves away from a total reliance on narrow, single variable experiments is moving nicely, thanks in large part to the
impetus given by Piaget and Vygotsky. The psychology of language and communication, the microanalysis of social psychology, all of these as they become more paradigmatic of the
ordinary begin to have a broader impact within and beyond
psychology. But what I also see, and I am deeply impressed
by it, is the extent to which comparable structural descriptions
in anthropology, sociology, linguistics and artificial intelligence
begin to make possible for us a more fruitful exchange.

The "exemplary" case of Sigmund Freud. Now, finally, why
Freud had such an impact on common sense. I think there are
three crucial points to make. Before I do so, however, let me
put in perspective one possible impediment to a proper appreciation. It has to do with his emphasis on sexuality, particularly
his insistence that it was not only ubiquitous but had its origins
in infancy. Undoubtedly this insistence (and particularly its
oversimplification in the hands of both admirers and detrac-
tors) did seize the imagination of educated and uneducated
alike. But had that been all, his views would have created a
frisson de scandale much as Havelock Ellis's had done, and
would soon have been converted to smut. His power in public
discussion had rather to do, I think, with these things: his
attention to and reinterpretation of the ordinary (the psycho-

pathology of everyday life, as he chose to call it), his deeply puzzling examination of the relation between the intended and the unintended, and finally his interpretation of the nature or meaning of "significance." A word about these.

For Freud, the ordinary conduct of everyday life was the starting point. Neurosis was not a blemish nor a disease, but a continuation of ordinary living. The ordinary, for Freud, was as much in need of interpretation as the extraordinary. One did what one intended to do, yes, but there was a hidden reason, a latent content as well as a manifest one. Intention, in Mrs. Anscombe's sense cited earlier, was reopened for examination. The Freudian slip became a tool for reinterpreting the ordinary.

But then, if the ordinary is not what it seems, what is it? Here is where Freud's literary genius took charge. Beneath the ordinary is a drama. Each of us is a cast of characters, acting out a script. Looked at carefully, our reactions to the world could be seen as an enactment of the script. It is in terms of these scripts that the surface of experience has systematic meaning or significance. Freud's scripts may have been culture-bound projections of *fin-de-siècle* Vienna. But for him they served as the cognitive systems in terms of which the symbolic significance of events could be understood. One of the scripts or codes was, of course, the epic struggle of the ego, the super-ego, and the id—the ego, as free agent trying to strike compromises between the priggish, societal demands of the superego on the one hand and the hedonistic, lusting, pleasure-principled id on the other. Indeed, he even tried his hand at a theory of perception in his essay on the "magic writing-pad" to account for the motivated way in which perceptual selectivity operated, balancing between a near-hallucinatory program in the service of drive and prohibition, and a reality-oriented one serving the sturdy little ego, almost like a judas eye through the middle of a distorting mirror. And as if these coding principles were not enough, Freud reinvented cultural forms like the Oedipal drama with its principles of categorization such that to the experiencer, every older man was a father, every older woman a mother, every ingratiation a denied parricide or a maternal seduction.

The ordinary, in a word, was to be understood as explicable in terms of its symbolic, coded value; coded values were to be understood in terms of the way in which the world was organized in secret thought below the surface; the response of society and of the self—whether indignation or anxiety or guilt—was to be understood in terms of the sharing of these codes. Memory, perception, action, motivation were all to be seen as structure-sensitive constituents of this overall operation. The system may have been plainly wrong in content and detail, may indeed (as we know from a decade or two of principally American experimental research to tame it) have been totally unamenable to test by controlled experiment of the kind representing the older positivism. But surely it represented a modern ideal and, in an abstract way, constituted the kind of explanation that we speak of as structurally systematic. Various writers have pointed out its similarities in this abstract sense to the theoretical programs of Chomsky, de Saussure, and Piaget—all of them based on the analysis of surface phenomena derived from underlying structures through the interposition of transformation rules—in Freud's case, dream work and the distortion of ego defense mechanisms were the principal transformations. Perhaps, as intellectual historians, we should take seriously the fact that this type of formulation has had so powerful an impact on common sense, on interpretations of the ordinary. The details of the Freudian drama have by now receded, but the approach in its formal character has become part of educated common sense.

Please do not misinterpret. I am not proposing that only those theories which have a general cultural impact be taken seriously. God save all counter-intuitive ideas! My claim, rather, is that educated human beings, given their intrinsic "science-making" or theory-making capacities, know how to do things and know that they do them. A theory of human behavior that fails to make contact with man's conceptions of his world and his way of knowing, that sets these aside as epiphenomena, will neither be an adequate theory of human behavior nor will it prevail in common sense. Physics had to make the world of nature, as experienced, comprehensible to man. The task of the psychologist is more difficult. For in making man comprehensible to himself, we start with man's knowledge of himself, his intricate sense of what he is like. Unless we begin from a better systematic description of that, we will fail. I doubt that we will, although our first century has not, I fear, been very impressive.